PENGUIN BOOKS

A WAVERING GRACE

'Elegant and moving ... Young's writing is limpid and the evocation of his memories of Vietnam, some bitter, some very sweet, is delightful and at times challenging' William Shawcross, *Sunday Times*

'This unusual book by a senior war reporter brought home the full atrocity and tragedy of Vietnam to me at last, along with a sense of the beauty of the place and its people ... The author witnesses the wild hysteria and hopeless confusion of the Tet Offensive of 1968, the police state horrors which followed the communist victory of 1975 and finally the peaceful but abjectly poor Vietnam of today' Andrew Barrow, *Spectator*

'An intriguing personal history ... a major contribution to our understanding of Vietnam' Andrew Rosenheim, *The Times Literary Supplement*

'A book as entertaining as his *Slow Boats to China* ... Young is an accomplished stylist ... [and] keeps up the suspense with dramatic slices of action and the occasional hilarious set piece' Sara Wheeler, *Daily Telegraph*

'[A] haunting evocation of the Vietnam War' Lucretia Stewart, *Guardian*

'He furnishes us with an extraordinary picture of how one society, within a single lifetime, can change and change again' Justin Wintle, *Literary Review*

D1589853

Gavin Young spent most of his youth in Cornwall and South Wales. He studied modern history at Oxford University and spent two years with a shipping company in Basra, Iraq, before setting out for wilder places. At first he lived with the Marsh Arabs in southern Iraq, between the Tigris and Euphrates rivers, and he recorded his adventures there in his first book, *Return to the Marshes*. He then stayed with the obscure people of the plains and mountains of south-western Arabia. From Tunis he joined the *Observer* as a foreign correspondent in 1960 and subsequently covered fifteen wars and revolutions throughout the world. He is a Fellow of the Royal Society of Literature.

Return to the Marshes (1977) was followed by *Iraq: Land of Two Rivers* (1980), an account of his journey through Mesopotamia. Gavin Young then travelled around the world, by whatever waterborne transport was available at the time, and published the story of that extraordinary voyage in his next two bestselling books, *Slow Boats to China* (1981) and *Slow Boats Home* (1985). A compilation of his writing appeared in 1987 as *Worlds Apart*, summoning up more than twenty years of travel and adventure in some of the world's most remote and exciting places. This was followed a year later by *Beyond Lion Rock*, relating the remarkable story of Cathay Pacific Airways. He continued his lifelong fascination with travel and his love of the sea in *In Search of Conrad* (1991), a magical evocation of the world of Joseph Conrad. In 1995 *From Sea to Shining Sea* was published, a present-day journey into America's past. Many of Gavin Young's books are published in Penguin. His latest, *Eye on the World*, is forthcoming from Viking.

A Wavering Grace

A VIETNAMESE FAMILY IN WAR AND PEACE

GAVIN YOUNG

PENGUIN BOOKS

PENGUIN BOOKS

Published by the Penguin Group
Penguin Books Ltd, 27 Wrights Lane, London W8 5TZ, England
Penguin Putnam Inc., 375 Hudson Street, New York, New York 10014, USA
Penguin Books Australia Ltd, Ringwood, Victoria, Australia
Penguin Books Canada Ltd, 10 Alcorn Avenue, Toronto, Ontario, Canada M4V 3B2
Penguin Books (NZ) Ltd, 182–190 Wairau Road, Auckland 10, New Zealand

Penguin Books Ltd, Registered Offices: Harmondsworth, Middlesex, England

First published by Viking 1997
Published in Penguin Books 1998
1 3 5 7 9 10 8 6 4 2

Copyright © Gavin Young, 1997
All rights reserved

The author and publishers would like to acknowledge
permission to quote from the following works:
Herbert Read, 'The End of a War' from
Selected Poems, published by Sinclair-Stevenson;
R. S. Thomas, 'The Echoes Return Slow' from
The Echoes Return Slow, published by Macmillan
General Books; Hugh MacDairmid, 'Lament for
Great Music' from Collected Poems,
published by Carcanet;
Thomas Hardy, 'After a Journey'
from The Complete Poems,
published by Papermac

The moral right of the author has been asserted

Printed in England by Clays Ltd, St Ives plc

Except in the United States of America, this book is sold subject
to the condition that it shall not, by way of trade or otherwise, be lent,
re-sold, hired out, or otherwise circulated without the publisher's
prior consent in any form of binding or cover other than that in
which it is published and without a similar condition including this
condition being imposed on the subsequent purchaser

No might can win against this wandering
wavering grace of humble men.

Herbert Read: *The End of a War*

This book is for

Mme Ngô Thi Bong

and all the other courageous and long-suffering mothers
and widows of Vietnam, North and South.

This was a face . . .
. . . that had seen love burn and lovers go forth
to the wars, and waited without hope, but without bitterness, for
someone worthy of it to return.

Am I catalyst of her mettle that,
at my approach, her grimace of pain
turns to a smile? What it is saying is:
'Over love's depths only the surface is wrinkled'.

R.S. THOMAS: 'The Echoes Return Slow'

Contents

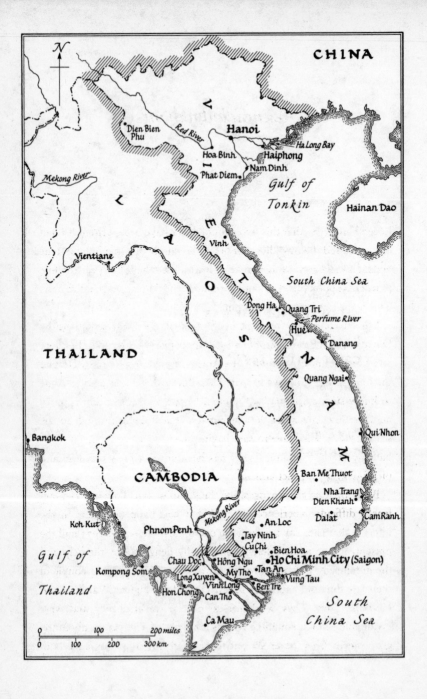

Acknowledgements

I need hardly say that this book could never have been written if I had not witnessed the tragedies that befell the family of Mme Bong in Hué and later in Saigon. More than that, it would not have been worthwhile putting the book together at all without having known them intimately. This is their story before it is mine.

What took me to Vietnam in the first place? I was sent there by David Astor, the then editor of my newspaper, *The Observer* of London, and I arrived just in time for the American invasion in 1965. Despite the horrors and sorrows of war, I was lucky that I was able to come to know such a country as Vietnam. I hope my love of that country and the quicksilver people who inhabit it will come through to the reader. All in all I have to say, having spent what seems like at least half my life in Vietnam, that it has been an enormous privilege and pleasure knowing Vietnamese.

Being there in the war was one thing. Going back later to Vietnam was a difficult experience after all that had happened there in the interim, that is to say between the communist victory of 1975 and the present. It was made tolerable and finally delightful by the help and the unfaltering welcome I received from two Vietnamese, a couple in their late thirties I had never set eyes on before: Nguyen Van Viet and his wife, Tam. They work for an official travel agency and were invaluable – not as sounding boards for views of Vietnamese about the government (they never set out to be that) but simply as experts in those fields of boring but necessary technicalities: getting visas, arranging flights and hotels; things like that. These are vital things not very easily arranged in Vietnam today. Luckily, Viet and Tam are also delightful people.

It may seem odd to thank a government which I have no reason to love – the communist government of Vietnam, I mean – for allowing me to return, not once or twice but several times in the last two years. In Hanoi, they might have looked on me as a menace, as someone who would try to overthrow the regime in some furtive way. Nothing was further from my thoughts, by the way. But how could they know that? I simply hoped against hope that the 'communism with a smiling face' which I saw around me, far from being sabotaged by hardliners, would last. True, I had fears that things might slip back to the appalling state of affairs that existed in 1985, when the dogmatic communists were in control, the time when I saw in Vietnam nothing but malice and decay. But things have changed for the better. I hope that in this book, despite the downside, I have made that positive side quite clear.

Things have changed for the better, I must add, not just for me but more importantly for most Vietnamese still in Vietnam. Though not much, alas, for Mme Bong, or the members of her family who were forced to flee as refugees after spending far too long in hard labour camps.

Some, but only *some*, passages in Parts One, Two and Four of this book have been taken from notes I made at the time the events I describe were happening, or just after they had happened: my dispatches to the London *Observer* were based on them, and in some cases these were reproduced in an earlier book consisting of purely journalistic dispatches. Despite this, I want to assure readers that by far the greater part of what is written here is quite new.

At home I must thank my new editor at Viking and Penguin, Peter Carson, and of course my wonderful 'sea anchor', Gritta Weil, who put this typescript together. To all those above and to other people mentioned in the text I am eternally grateful.

GAVIN YOUNG
Hué, Chiang Mai and London
January 1995–July 1996

Prelude

This is a strange, sad story, one that started a good while before my arrival on the Vietnamese scene, which was not until 1965.

So I never knew Vietnam during the French war, which ended in the disastrous surrender of 13,000 men of the French army at Dien Bien Phu in 1954; I never saw Saigon in its French colonial days – which some say was its best time; I never knew Hué when the last Emperor Bao Dai reigned over Annam; and I never knew Mme Bong in her youth, when she had lost her husband and for a time joined the Viet Minh independence fighters in the jungle. I haven't enough imagination to picture the pomp and ceremony in that extraordinary city, Hué, the traditional home of the Annamese emperors, where the last living emperor, Bao Dai, then the French-appointed Head of State, lived in the citadel in a palace built in imitation of the Forbidden City of Peking. Because I was not in Annam at the time I did not have to report to my newspaper the dire news that even there, even in his imperial capital, Hué, loyalty to Bao Dai had begun to wane noticeably in the last few years of the French colonial administration so that his popularity had dipped well below that of Ho Chi Minh. In retrospect I see that the 'problem' of Bao Dai would have been best expressed perhaps in Graham Greene's question: 'Did he, linked by education and self-interest to France, really desire the independence of his country if independence threatened the security of the royal domains – the palace in Dalat, the hunting lodge in Ban Me Thuot, the palace in Hué?'

Because the general 'problem' of Vietnam was all to do with Vietnamese independence: total independence from the French then; total independence from the Americans in my time.

When I was there, of course, the war was confined to the south of Vietnam: in the French time of Marshal de Lattre, the Foreign Legion, the Moroccans, the Algerians, the Senegalese, and those Vietnamese who fought for the French were mostly shuffled off to the north to defend the Red River Delta, to protect Hoa Binh and Hanoi, and to end up in the débâcle in the absurdly remote post of Dien Bien Phu; a débâcle fatal to the French, engineered almost as much by General Henri-Eugène Navarre, the French commander-in-chief, as by General Vo Nguyen Giap, the Viet Minh commander. I only recently learned that almost 70 per cent of the out-gunned garrison of Dien Bien Phu were colonial troops, not French at all.

I have been able only to read – obviously I got there too late to report it at the time – that many Vietnamese, particularly the peasants without any rights at all, felt long before the arrival of the American war machine that this was not their war. Their repeated argument was 'How can we fight until we have real independence? We have nothing to fight for.' Vietnam was not like Malaya in the 1950s, where the British fought a successful war against Chinese communist guerrillas and, while doing so, decided to grant the Malays complete independence. As a consequence of that the Malays had every reason to help the British to win. This, alas, was not the case in Vietnam, where General Giap, an ex-professor of history and geography before he became a successful revolutionary commander, had trained his fellow countrymen since 1945 to fight because true independence was far from being on the cards.

So the sound of the guns went drearily on until 'the wavering grace of humble men' finally won out, and the crippled and dead had multiplied, bringing the tally to (say) 3 million Vietnamese soldiers dead plus the uncounted number of civilians whose limbs were lopped off or who were disembowelled for, as far as they could see, no return at all. Add 58,000 Americans dead and others missing in action – leave alone the French casualties and, before them right at the end of the Second World War, the occupying Japanese. That's approximately what the Vietnam war cost in human terms.

I was too young to remember the youth of Ho Chi Minh and the making of the revolutionary leader that he became. So it comes as a revelation to find, as I did recently, that a senior French official, M. Sainteny, the first postwar Commissioner in Hanoi, wrote in his book, *Histoire d'une paix manquée*, that Ho Chi Minh in 1946 was disposed to concede to France the 'care of those things which she holds most dear': her economic and cultural interests. M. Sainteny – and he should have known – compared Ho Chi Minh to Gandhi in his reluctance to use force (a comparison that reads interestingly now). And, having negotiated with him in Hanoi, he quotes Ho as saying: 'If we wish to administer our own country, and if I ask you to withdraw your administrators, on the other hand I shall need your professors, your engineers, and your capital to build a strong and independent Vietnam.'

Now the rulers of Vietnam, independent at last although abjectly poor, are saying the same thing to all the world.

I try to picture Mme Bong's house in Hué – No. 103 Tran Hung Dao Street – as it was years ago, and the royal tombs as they were between the two World Wars. I never knew rue Catinat in Saigon in the days when French army officers or members of the Sûreté sat at the café tables drinking their flat-tasting vermouth-cassis while Colonel Thé, chief-of-staff of the Cao Daist forces fighting French and communists alike, planted his 200-lb bombs in a square in Saigon to explode among the shopping crowds. I only read the other day about General Bay Vien, who, when he controlled the gambling joints and opium parlours of Cholon, the Chinese city which is part of Saigon, cleared its streets of beggars by putting them, one-legged, armless, perhaps

3

broken-backed, into a squalid concentration camp. There were a number of loathsome South Vietnamese officers in my time, so I can imagine him without too much difficulty.

The American war in Vietnam fixed pictures in my mind that twenty or thirty years have been unable to wear away.

All in all it makes an ugly story, totally unrelieved, I suppose, if it were not for one or two absurd episodes in the daily life of a war correspondent. And of course for the delightful, infinitely patient Vietnamese people – the ordinary 'humble' people of 'wavering grace' in the paddy fields and the city streets, of North or South Vietnam, whom I am able to visit now in total peace for the first time.

Part One

RECOLLECTIONS OF WAR

We are professionals: we have to go on fighting
till the politicians tell us to stop. Probably they
will get together and agree to the same peace
that we could have had at the beginning, making
nonsense of all these years.

Graham Greene: *The Quiet American*

Chapter 1

The day I returned to Vietnam, checking into a new government hotel behind the central square of Saigon that was so familiar to me, was one of the happiest of my life. It was only when Mme Bong's grandson Vu said to me, 'Qué and his family are coming today for the last time. They take the plane to America', that I realized that my Vietnam story was going to have a very tangled – in fact, a hopelessly sad-sweet – ending.

Vu had driven from the tiny house in the remote suburb of Saigon Mme Bong had moved into when she was forced by the communists to move from her home in Hué sometime after 1985. His old motorbike was propped against the kerb outside the hotel ready to take me there. When I had been to see Mme Bong soon after I returned, she had promised to invite Qué's family for a last lunch to meet me. 'There's not much time left,' she had warned. 'Soon he'll be gone.'

I hadn't seen Qué for over twenty-three years – since before the war ended, in fact. Now, about to see him again, apparently for the last time in Vietnam, I thought bitterly, 'One meeting in twenty-three years is not enough.' It seemed hardly fair that my old friend was leaving Vietnam for good almost at the very moment I got back.

How could any ending be happy for the survivors of a thirty- or forty-year war that for them culminated in seven years' imprisonment, and then, after release, unemployment and final exile, not to mention the poverty, the dashed hopes of a whole lifetime, and the humiliation?

Hearing Vu's words, I expected to find Qué sitting distraught among his few remaining belongings, ready for his family's departure for the United States, about to go – for ever – into an exile he dreaded. Years ago, I knew, he had applied to the United Nations refugee people in Saigon and the Vietnamese communist authorities for permission to escape, wanting desperately to find sanctuary for his wife and children as much as for himself – any sanctuary at all. Unluckily the ageing communist leaders in Hanoi were going through an unremittingly vindictive phase towards non-communists – and this inhuman and economically suicidal policy was to last more than ten years after their victory in 1975. So the horror was that when at long last Qué's permission came through, Vietnam had once more become a reasonable place to live in; yet for him it was too late. He could not withdraw his application to leave. He no longer wanted, or needed, to go. Yet now he had no alternative.

Dang Van Qué (from now on I shall continue to call him Qué) had been my friend for exactly thirty years. I met him when I was covering the war in Vietnam for my London newspaper. I visited his home town, Hué, in central Vietnam in 1965, ten years before the communists won the war against the Americans and entered Saigon.

Qué was a Buddhist, like most people in Hué. And, like Buddhists there and in Hué's sister-city Danang, he didn't care for the loud and pushy Americans, he loathed and despised the corrupt and incompetent generals and colonels who ruled in Saigon with America's approval, and he disliked almost everything he had heard about the communists of the North. He was, I suppose, a pure Vietnamese nationalist. But war being war, he was called up willy-nilly into the army and when the victorious communists entered Saigon in 1975, Qué – a shy, retiring intellectual, the sort of man who might in the West have registered as a conscientious objector – found himself rounded up with all those generals and colonels and bundled off to a 're-education camp', as the

8

communists called the isolated places they set aside for their prisoners of war. There this timid, thoughtful and blameless man in his mid-twenties was locked up for seven and a half years; labelled 'a criminal'; shut off from the world; far from his family (he had just married), and isolated from his friends. He was, however, not 're-educated' as the communists had intended. (Nor do I know of anyone who was.)

Qué is highly literate. Though his parents were among the poorest of the poor, he made it his business to be well read in Vietnamese and French literature, being, as he is, part of a generation of Vietnamese who speak French as its second language as English is the second language of most Vietnamese now. One of my earliest memories of the unpretentious Bong family house where Qué lodged in Hué was a French version of Tolstoy's novel *War and Peace* on a window-sill in an upper room. It could not have belonged to either of Mme Bong's sons: neither Van nor Minh read books as far as I knew. It must have belonged to Qué. A copy (again in French) of Camus's *Le Mythe de Sisyphe* lay nearby, and Qué used to quote from it. A passage he particularly liked went:

> *'Est-ce-que le globe terrestre est bel?'*
> *'Oui. Très bel.'*

Those two lines of dialogue will always remind me of Qué.

During what was left of the twenty years since the end of the war and my longed-for return in 1995 to an utterly changed Vietnam – greatly changed for the better, of course – we had exchanged letters. Although when I saw him again the other day for the last time in Saigon, Qué told me that because of all the many years of official suspicion and strict censorship of the mail he had received only one or two of mine. I know I received two at the most of his. I was not surprised at that, though I was disappointed because I knew he desperately needed encouragement. One of my purposely encouraging letters to him contained a passionate plea not to give up hope. 'Please,' I had written, 'please, Qué, remember Camus's *Sisyphe* and the passage you used to recite to me.' I repeated the two lines of dialogue and went on: 'Remember that one day, my dear Qué, you will have a chance to see the globe, however unlikely that may seem now – and you will see for yourself that it *is* as Camus told you, "*Très bel*".' That letter never reached him. Qué told me that at our long-delayed reunion in Saigon, and to show me he hadn't forgotten *Sisyphe* he repeated those two lines of Camus.

'*Oui. Très bel*,' he said at last in a trembling voice and, with emotion, added, 'You don't forget anything, do you, Gavin?'

'One doesn't forget things like that,' I said. 'Or times like that.' And I thought, 'You are going to see part of that *globe terrestre* on your flight to Washington, D.C.'

After a pause, to lighten the mood, I said as briskly as I could, 'You're off very soon. What have you got left to do?'

'A few vaccinations. Well, a lot of those as a matter of fact.'

'Vaccinations? Against what?'

'Oh, I don't know,' Qué said. 'Against diseases of one sort or another. There seem to be an awful lot.'

'What diseases? Malaria? AIDS?'

'No! No!' they all laughed and the tension was broken for the moment. But it was a tension that never entirely disappeared, I am afraid. When I mentioned that his sons would have an exciting new life in the United States, the bleak mood descended again.

Qué shrugged and said, 'Well, I hope they will.' Taking my arm as if he wanted to confide a secret, he led me to the window. 'I have to tell you the truth,' he whispered, 'personally I just feel tired, really *tired*. Too damned tired to care about anything any more.'

I looked at him in silence; I could see the utter exhaustion in his eyes. There didn't seem much I could say. I looked silently at the sad, lined face, the thin, vulnerable neck and the wisps of hair on the middle-aged skull – and the sunken eyes. I thought of the quiet, cheerful young man I had known in Hué thirty years ago and I put my arm across his shoulders to comfort him.

'Since I came back here, I have been thinking,' I said at last. 'All those years ago the Buddhists of Hué, people like the monk Thich Tri Quang, the student leader Buu Ton, you yourself and your friend Minh – all of you – you wanted free elections and a negotiated peace. Remember? Well, if you'd got what you wanted then, it might have saved you all from the horrors that you had to put up with later: Tet 1968, the massacres, prisons, all the rest. But, of course, the Americans and the people in charge in Saigon said you were communists and traitors.'

Qué's answer startled me. With a sudden, bitter intensity he spat out, 'That's your conclusion, is it? An objective observer's conclusion?' He sounded as if he was addressing an enemy.

The trouble was I was not sure that it *was* my conclusion. Had peace really been possible at that moment? 'No, Qué,' was all I could say. 'I sit here with you and Mme Bong now, so many years after all that – and I only *think* it is. All we know for certain is that three million or so Vietnamese died here. Thousands more are in exile, and you are going to join them.' I smiled bleakly, 'Look, I don't know the answer. I don't even know the question.' In the same intense voice and with his eyes staring at the carpet, Qué said, 'There is only one question one can ask after all that's happened. And it can be summed up in one word.'

'What word is that, Qué?'

'The word is *"pourquoi?"*,' he replied. 'That is the word.'

Pourquoi? Why?

The very same word had struck me only the day before. Driving in a taxi past the walls of the former wartime American embassy, my driver had told me that the Stars and Stripes would be hoisted over it again in the near future: the old embassy would house the new American consulate-general in Saigon, he said. So, twenty years after the shameful scramble on the roof of the embassy that all the world saw on television, twenty years after terrified Vietnamese, hoping to be flown to safety, swarmed round the last American helicopters and were punched and kicked off them by desperate embassy staff, after 3 million Vietnamese had died, the Americans (the taxi driver was confirming it to me) would be back as if nothing had happened. Meanwhile one man's, Qué's, life was in ruins. As Qué himself, on the verge of tears, had asked me – *Why?* What, in God's name, *had* been the point of it all? What could I have replied? 'Search me?'

In Graham Greene's novel of the French Indochinese War, *The Quiet American*, published in 1955, he makes a French officer say, 'But we are professionals: we have to go on fighting till the politicians tell us to stop. Probably they will get together and agree to the same peace that we could have had at the beginning, making nonsense of all these years.' And that is what happened.

What had been the point?

Another memory of the horrific past came back to me. On 4 April 1975, very near the war's end, a big United States Air Force Lockheed C-5A jet, just after taking off from Tan San Nhat airport, Saigon, disintegrated in mid-air and crashed. It was a mercy flight. The crash killed 172 people, including seventy-eight Vietnamese children – orphans, I think – who were being evacuated to San Francisco, where President Ford was to meet them. The war was almost over by then. Soon communist forces would be 'liberating' Saigon, and they were blamed at first for shooting the plane down. But – at long last – the state of the aircraft was found to have left something to be desired and Lockheed paid out millions of dollars in compensation.

I read the other day that some of the dead children – what remains of them – are buried in a graveyard in southern Thailand where once American troops in Vietnam had a Rest and Recreation Centre. A frangipani tree shelters them, and it is fitting, I suppose, that in Thai the name for the frangipani blossoms is *lan thom*, the flower of death. Thais, I remembered, warn you not to bring them into the house.

Qué, of course, would hardly have noticed that tragedy. He had troubles enough of his own just then: after all, he was scared to death, about to be arrested and would go to jail for seven years. His life was beginning to disintegrate just as that American aircraft had done.

One could only repeat to oneself Qué's question: *pourquoi?* What *was* the point of it? Today at Mme Bong's, Qué had brought a plastic bag of red roses as a present for me. I was glad that at least they were not *lan thom*: and after all I am grateful that I was permitted this brief 'hail and farewell' before the KLM jet bore him away into exile from the Vietnam he was preparing to love again, from the Vietnam that had so changed. If he stayed he would never have to relive the humiliations and senseless persecutions of the last two decades. Those horrors and the horrors of the long war: aerial bombardments by the Americans, napalm attacks, My Lai massacres, defoliation and mass graves – all these things have ended for good. So has Hanoi's exclusive 'jobs for the communist boys' policy, the midnight arrests, the searching of houses at all hours, the barking and the bullying by communist cadres whose faces had been distorted into ugliness by years of anger and contempt.

That was the irony in Qué's fate.

There was no possibility of a change of plans. The airline ticket was issued – for himself, for his two boys, for his small daughter and his wife; the passports and visas were in order; the medical checks had been completed. The plane was due to leave for Kuala Lumpur, Amsterdam and New York in a few days. There was no escape.

Qué had even sold the tiny slum house out at Bien Hoa he had lived in since his release from the prison camp. He had never owned very much, and now with the house sold he owned nothing but the clothes he stood up in. For his last few days he and his family were lodging with Mme Bong, his benefactress from Hué. Her own children and grandchildren were already in the United States as refugee boat people, studying and working in Virginia, not very far from Washington, D.C. – where Qué would end up.

One more thing contributed to the sadness of Qué's plight: he doesn't speak English well. He has spoken Vietnamese or French nearly all his life, and by now at his age – he is about fifty – he is unlikely to learn American-English, a fact that will make exile even more dire. He has heard me warning his two sons that they will have to concentrate all their efforts on becoming word-perfect in their new tongue if they are to get on in the competitive world of job-getting. Without perfect American, I told them, they will never – if then – be able to find total satisfaction in the American way of life. Qué agrees, with his sad smile. 'It's important for them,' he says, emphasizing the 'them'. 'But you know, it's far too late for *me* to learn a new language.' I am afraid he is right.

For the sake of his children at least, he has to go. The idea of America thrills them. I saw them at Mme Bong's obscure house almost hopping with excitement at the prospect of taking that plane to a new life in America, the home of Sylvester Stallone and McDonald's hamburgers. Not to go now would risk deeply disappointing them.

Eating spring rolls and noodles in Mme Bong's front room, I was struck again by another ironic upshot of the new liberalization. On this visit I could go at will from my hotel in central Saigon to visit Mme Bong's house in the city's western suburbs – I had already done so on several occasions and I had done so today. I was as free on this visit to come and go between my hotel and her house as I would have been in England or Singapore. Or Washington, D.C., for that matter. Ten years ago I had been sternly warned not to see her or any of her family.

I hoped Qué would survive the long flight; he looked terribly old and thin. He had had a weak chest for years (or was it a dicky heart?). Whatever it was, I tried to convince him to see a doctor in America as soon as he could. He said he would, with the familiar faint smile and the vague nod of his head that assured me of nothing.

I left Vietnam for Bangkok just before Qué and his family flew to America. I intended to be back in Saigon in a month or two, but he wouldn't be here. I was left longing to hear news of his arrival in America. I was in Thailand when about a month later his first letter arrived from Washington – in French, of course.

It read:

We arrived in Washington, D.C., on 22 February at 9 o'clock in the evening. Three weeks have passed. My wife is beginning her new job in an hotel. My two sons are going to work too, and my little daughter goes to school near our apartment.

I myself have become quite useless in this 'new life' of ours, and this feeling has haunted me from the first day here. To tell the truth, I must get used to the shame of being here. I have nothing to regret, but at the same time there is nothing to fill the void which I feel in my soul.

This morning, I stand at the window of the apartment watching people pass in the street below. It is a fine day and I think of you in Thailand . . .

At the end of the letter he added his new address and telephone number in Washington, D.C. He wrote his name, too. Changed, of course. His Americanized name will be Que Van Dang. No accent. Later I expect it will become simply Que Dang.

The letter is signed 'Your friend, Qué', and it strikes me as one of the saddest I have ever received.

It reads like a letter from someone beginning not a new life, but a life sentence.

Chapter 2

My quaint recollection is – and my photographs (only slightly out of focus) bear me out – that Qué and Mme Bong, when I saw them on my return to Saigon, looked almost the same age, almost like husband and wife. A bizarre impression, I know, because there is something like twenty-five years' difference in age between them.

I know the reason, of course. It is simply the brutal war and its soul-destroying aftermath. Qué's nervous face shows in every line his years of suffering, mental as much as physical. The caved-in cheeks in the poet's face, the melancholy expression, the unfocused gaze, the long silences, come from the same source. Adversity had changed him more than it has changed Mme Bong. It is in his nature.

As for Mme Bong, she has been through God knows what anguish for much longer but still manages to look as impassive as when I first met her thirty years ago. Mme Bong lost her husband in the time of the war between the Viet Minh and the French colonial regime in the 1950s so, with her, the vale of tears goes back a long way. Indomitable is the word that would once have been applied to such an extraordinary woman: unfailingly indomitable. And unfailingly generous, too. That she is the soul of kindness I have not doubted since I was first welcomed as a guest in her house in Hué in 1965. She had already taken in Qué's parents with their children, out of sheer goodness of heart. Qué's family was poverty-stricken, and both his father and his mother were illiterate. His father (I remember a small friendly man with white hair) rolled cheap cigarettes on the sidewalk outside Mme Bong's house on Tran Hung Dao Street, selling them to earn a basic income although, of course, he and his wife ate and slept inside at Mme Bong's. Their son Qué was brought up and went to school with Mme Bong's second son, Minh, who became my friend and first led me to his mother's house.

The house was certainly no palace. Its entrance was a shop front in a long street of shop fronts. It was narrow, but very deep: it ran back a long way. I remember scars on the walls, and a fat, clucking hen stalking about the downstairs room with her chicks, and there was hopelessly indecisive wiring, some of it seemingly unattached to anything at all. The house had – originally – two storeys. I remember an electric fan showering bright particles of dust over us all, an old woman sweeping, slowly and vaguely, slop-slopping in sandals across the stone floor. In the outer hallway, which had been turned into a tailor's shop, small boys stitched away, making name tabs, sitting bent over their work in cotton shorts and plastic sandals. One such boy – perhaps he had been on night shift – gathered up his red bedroll and mat, went to a tap and brushed his teeth with amazing care: very slowly and very long. He winked when he saw me watching him and returned with his mat and bedroll to the tailors.

Food was never a problem. Mme Bong put noodles on the table; hot cucumber soup followed, and a dish of small flaming hot red chillis; then came a hunk of some large white fish, a salad, boiled rice, a chopped omelette and green peppers. And finally there was tea. The family attacked the meal with flying chopsticks as if they had never seen food before. But I was always chided by Mme Bong: 'You, the biggest! And you eat so little. We are poor – perhaps you don't like Vietnamese food?' Of course I protested. I did like Vietnamese food – very much, as it happens – and still do. It was just that I was always too excited to eat much in Hué. I had found a new world which attracted me. Even the Vietnamese language, which I never could learn, quacked out by these Hué people, entranced me. Greene, in my view, was wrong when, in *The Quiet American*, he described some Vietnamese as whispering 'like crooners, in their language like a song'. Vietnamese seldom whisper and they sound to me more like charming ducks: their monosyllabic language came out in a series of sweet quacks. Not that I minded. Then, Mme Bong and her family always spoke to me in French. Mme Bong does so to this day.

I made notes in 1965 of all I could learn about the habits, the likes and dislikes of the typical Hué student.

He liked the films of the British pop star Cliff Richard (the Beatles came later), and adored anything that smacked of love or tragedy in films or books. On their walls they liked to pin up posters showing romantic country scenes from places which they thought they would never visit, like Switzerland: a cottage by a waterfall, snow-covered hills and probably a deer or two wandering among pine trees. The average student's home was surprisingly dirty (though Mme Bong's house, not being one, was spotless) and a good many cigarette ends were scattered around on the floor. Yet personally the students looked impeccably clean and their cheap clothes were well scrubbed: jeans usually, and long-sleeved shirts with the sleeves rolled up. They were a sentimental lot, and so intensely keen to learn that they tried to copy everything you said. They were very poor, yet they possessed a few much-prized objects: a radio, a scooter, perhaps four shirts, and two pairs of trousers. They yearned for a scholarship and to travel. In those days French was still taught in the schools, and most students spoke it (including Minh and Qué), but English looked like catching up.

Above all, the Vietnamese boy and girl students of Hué were extremely likeable; lovable, one might easily say.

That was my impression of young men and girls all those years ago in the capital of Annam, at the beginning of the last horrendous decade of war.

These days, I suppose, few are left alive or, if alive, are still in Vietnam. Those who were not disembowelled or vaporized by bombs and rockets, or did not go off with the North Vietnamese Army, or were not raped and murdered by Thai pirates fleeing into exile, or were not drowned when their leaky boats capsized and lie now at the bottom of the South China Sea – those who survived all these dreadful ends are living as exiles, as *Viet Kieu* (overseas Vietnamese), in America, Australia, or Britain or France, or in a dozen other countries.

The chances are that they will never see their homeland again.

Mme Bong welcomed me almost as if I was a member of her family when I was first introduced to her by Minh and Qué when they were still students of about seventeen or eighteen. I soon came to appreciate her enormous strength and character. She exuded strength – in her ramrod back, in her piercing, fearless gaze, for example. And strong she had to be, for this diminutive woman with high cheekbones, who swept back her hair and was always proud to dress in her Vietnamese clothes – the white silk trousers, the long tight jacket with a slit up the thigh (it is called an *ao dai*) – has had much trouble to put up with from the moment I intruded into her family circle. Though I must add that the trouble was nothing to do with my presence.

The first thing to try her were the Buddhist 'peace' riots in Hué and Danang. Being young and hotheaded Buddhists, Minh and his brother Van became deeply involved, even defying their mother.

I was new to Hué and what I remember of the riots comes back in flashes as if the whole alarming episode had taken place in a storm illuminated by lightning.

The comings and goings in Hué at that time were intense. Young Vietnamese I had never seen before ran excitedly in and out of Mme Bong's house continually, some evidently carrying messages. Minh, Qué and Van, too, rushed eagerly about as if a crisis in the war had been reached, as if the North Vietnamese and the Viet Cong were about to withdraw and the Americans about to abandon their protégés, the greedy generals in Saigon. One morning I found Minh oiling a carbine in the family hallway, and I knew things had taken a turn for the worse. Surely, I thought, the Buddhist students were not actually going to start shooting South Vietnamese soldiers in the streets of Hué? It looked very much like it – and in fact this very thing happened. Egged on by a respected monk called Thich Tri Quang and other senior monks of Hué, Minh and his student friends actually took to the streets, erected barricades in Hué and in Danang, where the Americans had a large base, and prepared seriously to fire on troops sent up from Saigon in American aircraft. It was as bad as that; and perhaps this upheaval in the South gave the communists in Hanoi the impression that the people of Hué and central Vietnam were hoping for a communist victory. As a matter of fact, nothing could have been farther from the truth; Minh and his friends (by now openly in arms and wearing Buddhist scarves round their necks) were convinced that communism was barbaric and malign, just as they considered the Americanization of their country degrading. Strangely enough – that is, to outsiders, including unfortu-nately the Americans – they merely desired the means to wage a more *successful* war against the communists. For they believed that the American-sponsored generals who ruled the country were hopelessly corrupt and incompetent. And they wanted – they repeated it *ad nauseam* – free and fair elections, a popular civilian government and an end to that American-sponsored corruption which they thought was playing into the hands of the communist leaders in Hanoi. They were, in my view at least, pure Vietnamese nationalists, proud of their history and their culture. They feared and mistrusted foreign influences of any kind.

The desires of the Buddhist people of Hué were spelt out to me by Buu Ton, the young leader of the Buddhist students there.

'We know the communist Front is controlled by the North,' he said. 'If we had a popular government, it would be able to give our forces permission to bomb the North – or it could decide not to. As it is, the American Seventh Fleet picks targets at will, with no reference to us, or anybody else for that matter.'

The middle-aged rector of Hué university disagreed with him and impatiently dismissed the students, saying, 'Youngsters don't know what they talk about. There is no sign that Hanoi wants peace.' That, as far as I knew, was true. But supposing, I thought, Hanoi didn't want peace because of the growing American presence in the South. Suppose they would want peace once the foreigners had gone, and negotiations could then take place with the 'neutralist' Buddhists and Catholics and other non-communist members of an elected government? Wouldn't that be a good thing? At least something worth trying?

It was a confusing situation. Mme Bong kept out of the bellicose comings and goings in her house, only pausing now and again to verbally chastise her son Minh. 'Pull yourself together, Minh. You're just like your father. Always rushing into impossible situations.' Once she seized his carbine out of his unprotesting hands and thrust it into a drawer, saying, 'Let's get rid of *that* thing for a start.' I think Qué, in spite of his close friendship with Minh, agreed with her desire to play things down.

I have just come across a communiqué issued by the Buddhist Struggle Group leader, the monk Thich Tri Quang. Put out in Hué in April 1966, it is marked, rather pompously like an official document: 'Unclassified'.

The extracts I quote from it here are important to anyone who was in Vietnam at the time, because they set out quite plainly – well, as plainly as the hesitant translation could make it plain – a good many of the demands Buddhists were trying to insist on, and the reason for that insistence.

First of all, I would like to let you know that when the Buddhist Association decided to fight for a national assembly, this did not mean that the Association wanted to get involved in politics. We all know that our blood and bones were sacrificed in the overthrow of a regime which only knew how to discriminate against people – the regime of [the Catholic dictator] Diem. And what did we get? Only governments which did not have a constitution or national assemblies which were established and then overthrown. We, sometimes, were forced to hold demonstrations against the Government because of their betrayals.

We kept our temper [at times] so that they could have a chance to regain their honor in order to serve the nation [by 'they' he meant the present government of General Thieu, for example]. But there were only betrayals, not only in plans in their minds, but in their actions and implementations.

So what should we do? We cannot just demonstrate against the Government, from this Government to another Government, to be betrayed again and again. We would be demonstrating against the Government every six months.

We must have a national assembly. We have our right to vote so that a future Government will be formed by the national assembly. If that Government betrays us, it will betray us to a fixed degree, for a fixed time. Buddhists, who have sacrificed their blood and bones during these years, cannot live in a country which does not have a national assembly or is controlled by Washington. We hope to have a national assembly which can be run by Catholics, Cao Daists, Buddhists, or whoever; an assembly whose function will be clarified by a constitution with specified powers. When this point is reached, no one will be forced to ask the people to demonstrate against the government. This helps you understand why a national assembly is so important to us.

As for the Americans, Thich Tri Quang had this to say:

Any nation, when coming into another nation to help or to rule it – through its aid – the first thing and the last thing it will try to do is to annihilate the right of the local people to control their government. It will use local soldiers as mercenaries. A national assembly must be approved by a foreign country. As the world may know, we are oppressed by two pressures – the communists and the Americans. We must regain our right of self-determination, the right of electing our own national assembly.

Tri Quang's views on America's Vietnamese friends he expressed as follows:

Nguyen Van Thieu said he had signed a decree convening a national assembly, and that will be on August 15 . . . Here are our two choices: should we protest against Thieu and Ky and force them to withdraw; or should we try to maintain them in the national assembly, while controlling them in such a way that they cannot take advantage of their position or powers? They hold powers and means in their hands, and with these they could stymie the national assembly.

What should we do? Should we force Thieu and Ky to resign? I want you to think about this carefully. I would like to ask our political leaders to meet again in order to make a choice. Either they will overthrow Thieu and Ky or try to control them in such a way so that they cannot sway the national assembly. This will be done by Buddhists: by the People's Revolutionary Struggle Force, by the Students Revolutionary Struggle Force, etc. Know that we – the people and the soldiers of I Corps [the military region round Hué] are not afraid of bombs and weapons the Government threaten to use to oppress us – we make up our own minds. Thieu and Ky may send their airplanes or armoured cars here any time they want to by means of the foreigners' [Americans'] airplanes, but we are not afraid. We will always maintain our struggle spirit, and we must direct it in such a way as to avoid causing chaos. I will stay here with you because I know that sooner or later Thieu and Ky will bomb and shell here. That is the reason I must be with you.

This was his last word:

Thieu, Ky and the foreigners [the Americans again, of course] are trying to cause chaos. [I think 'perpetuate incompetence' is a better translation of what he was trying to say.] We must unite closely in order to say to the central government that we have a national assembly, and we will not let them take advantage of chaos in order to betray our right and that of the people. Everyone should return to his normal activity in order to protest against Thieu and Ky more strongly. We are living under a corrupt regime, and airplanes and armored cars may come at any time.

It is too easy to fight each other as we hold our demonstrations against the Government.

I pray that you will be wise and patient, in order to protect the nation and the Kharma.

I was certainly going to have to send a dispatch about the Buddhist brouhaha in Hué and Danang to my newspaper in London. And Thich Tri Quang was in Hué. Accordingly, one morning I jumped on one of Minh's old bicycles and, with him and his friend Vua on two other ancient bicycles, pedalled to Thich Tri Quang's pagoda across the river to see him. It was a sweltering hot day. On the uphill way to the temple on the old bike, which was far too small for me, I was glad to hear Vua's suggestion. 'Let's stop at this stall, Gavin,' he panted. '*Mon Dieu*, it's so hot.'

I would have agreed if I had had the breath. And we pulled up at a stall on the roadside and drank glass after glass of iced coconut juice.

Afterwards we staggered, sweating, into the pagoda's main yard. It was very quiet there; among trees a bell tinkled and pale-faced novice monks with the shaven heads and traditional topknots glided silently about. The source of the excitement that had thrown central Vietnam into such confusion might be in this temple but, I thought, you would never know it from the calm that reigned here.

We mopped our brows and waited in a sort of ante-room, shedding our shoes at the door, and at last were led in to meet the monk whose face had become familiar to me from the newspaper photographs. We squatted in front of him, Minh on one side of me, Vua on the other.

Thich Tri Quang was apparently unaffected by the heat. He had a large head and a white, cold face that was at the same time strangely sensuous, but he was not the horror to look at – the image of Yul Brynner playing Dracula had struck me – that he had often appeared in press photos. He spoke quickly and rather softly in Vietnamese, which I do not understand, and as he spoke his hands fluttered before him. Sometimes he chewed sweets, and sometimes he picked his bare feet, gazing over our heads. He was certainly withdrawn, and certainly proud. One could see that at least to himself – and his many followers – he was the embodiment of Vietnamese sovereignty; one could also see that American appeals to him to postpone political agitation until the war was won – some Americans then, I noted, talked of this happening within five years, ten at the most – were most unlikely to wash. Even then the end of the war seemed an aeon away – and an American victory over the communists was far from certain.

Nevertheless Tri Quang did not seem to resent my presence in his temple, and although an obviously proud man, he had a mischievous sense of humour. At every humorous sally – there were many – his attendants, squatting on the floor behind him, rocked with laughter, and so did Minh and Vua. He appeared to me as a sort of smaller Vietnamese version of Charles de Gaulle, and what he said was in essence – according to the respectful if muddled translations given me by Minh and Vua – all that his communiqué had said. I can't say I was taken with the man himself, but I couldn't help agreeing with most of what he had to say. Above all, I had come to the conclusion that neither the Buddhist Struggle Movement in Hué nor its leader, Thich Tri Quang, were communist stooges playing Hanoi's game and secretly praying for a communist victory. That some American officials in Saigon thought or pretended to think they were, underlined the fact that as well as being physical misfits in the small quicksilver world of Vietnam, Americans were also *political* misfits – something I feared might turn out to be a much more serious failing.

More impressions by flashes of lightning.

Sometime after the beginning of the Buddhist disturbances, I was sleeping as usual on a mat on a hard bed of Mme Bong's house, and woke up with a start in the early hours disturbed by a series of shattering explosions. The ground quaked; the house trembled; the sky flashed. Was it an earthquake? No, clearly bombs were falling.

I must add a word about what it was like to wake up in Mme Bong's house at that time.

The house was very dark at the best of times and ran back a long way from the street – it was divided up as far as I could see by a series of three-ply partitions. I slept (or rather, tried to sleep) on the plain, flat Vietnamese bed with no mattress and only a thin woven mat between the hard wood of the bed and my aching bones. Every joint in my body seemed to stick out and I became badly bruised whichever way I turned or twisted. In such circumstances to get up in the early morning was the usual sort of small agony – but worse. If the air was cold, the floor was icy; and to pad on bare feet down the creaking wooden stairs in one's underwear was a kind of freezing nightmare. It had to be done: the walk downstairs and along the splintered duckboards that led to the small agony of the bathhouse – a massive tub of cold water behind a wooden partition, the scoop beside it to enable one to pour the water over one's head and body, shivering and shaking, a shuddering mass of goose-pimples. It was worse than the compulsory cold baths in wintertime at school which our headmaster used to assure us were so bracing. The water was so cold the soap would barely lather. The skimpy towel, the only thing available at Mme Bong's to dry oneself on, was barely adequate; nor was the broken mirror one peered into to comb one's dripping hair much better. To go through all that in the semi-dark and a hurry, while bombs were falling somewhere in the city, was not merely bracing: it was agonizing.

That morning Minh, Qué, Van and Mme Bong were awake already, craning out of the upper windows. They had no idea what was happening, although it soon became evident that heavy mortar bombs had been launched at the little unimportant airstrip behind the citadel. Who could be responsible? No one knew, although everyone had an opinion. Some blamed the Viet Cong; others (mostly Buddhists) said the Americans were responsible, seeking ways to provoke demonstrations they could put down by force; some said it was the anti-Tri Quang, anti-communist Vietnamese Nationalist Party – the Kuomintang of Vietnam – up to its tricks, blaming the Buddhists.

All in all it was a typical Hué muddle. No one found out who really was responsible; everybody accused everybody else. Such was the state of things in 1966 in Hué. It demonstrated, I said in another piece to my newspaper, the determination on the part of Vietnamese of all classes and all religions, at least at this stage of the war, to divine hideously Machiavellian plottings behind any event whatsoever.

*

One scene will be forever lodged in my mind.

It was dark; a night of clouds and impending rain after the heat and humidity. Minh, Qué and Minh's elder brother, Van, and I were perched on the sill of Mme Bong's upper floor looking down on the street below. There, bedlam reigned: a violent demonstration. Already a long column of Buddhist students, armed with scarves with the Buddhist colours round their necks, had marched by, and now they were followed by some soldiers in uniform – locals, I presumed, and followers of Thich Tri Quang. Forming up down the road by the market on the other side of the street we could just see scores of children of roughly eight to fourteen years old. Another large group, the trishaw drivers, blank-eyed elderly men with fiery faces who looked (whether they did or not) as if they habitually drank methylated spirits and had amazingly hard, stringy legs, were due to pass beneath us, too; and then a ragged band of wild-haired, elderly women – like the *tricoteuses* of the French Revolution – who worked heaven knows where, would add their anger to the general fury. They chewed betel and so looked particularly daunting; their mouths were blood red as though they had just eaten their babies.

When most of the trishaw drivers had passed below, someone waving a flaming torch happened to look up. At once I was spotted – there was a foreigner up there, he shouted, pointing, possibly an American! The cry was taken up: 'A foreigner! An American!' The rowdiest part of the crowd looked ready to plunge into Mme Bong's house and set it ablaze. Alarmed, I suddenly thought, 'Am I going to be the cause of Mme Bong's family, her house, Mimi, her dog, and Mme Bong herself going up in flames – me, Gavin Young, her guest in Hué.' A fine thing!

I began to draw back out of sight. Too late. It was prompt action by Van which saved an ugly situation. He boldly stood up in his new uniform (he had just joined the army) and appealed to the crowd, by then hysterical to the point of murder.

'This man,' he cried, pointing straight at me, 'is our friend. Not an

American at all. An Englishman. He is the friend of all this house, of all of us here. He belongs to our family. Continue your march. We are all with you. We are *from* Hué and *for* Hué.'

It was a brave, and even a noble gesture. The crowd calmed down, the leaders picked up the step, and the march continued normally. One or two people even waved up at us in a friendly fashion.

'Phew!' said Qué later. 'You know, those old women are dangerous.' He was quite serious when he added, 'They beat you to death with their slippers.'

I think it was at that precise moment that I decided to try from then on to see the situation in Vietnam primarily through Vietnamese eyes and, while not neglecting the military aspects of the war (I went on several hair-raising operations in the interior with American, Australian and South Vietnamese units until I left the country in 1974), I tried to translate into print how the war affected them. Vietnam was their country, after all.

As Tri Quang had predicted, to put down the Buddhist riots – 'communist-inspired' riots, the Saigon official newspapers said – government troops were dispatched from the capital to central Vietnam (Danang and Hué). For the first time some of the many American journalists in Saigon were surprised to find that their soldiers – the American 'invasion' of Vietnam had begun the year before – were not universally loved or welcomed as saviours by all the people of South Vietnam, certainly not in the former imperial Annamese city of Hué. (It was during these riots that Buddhist monks again publicly burned themselves to death in the streets of Saigon.)

Soon after this came another blow. The same year as his son Vu was born, Van, Mme Bong's elder son, was killed in action with the South Vietnamese forces near Qui Nhon, and Mme Bong went down there, although Qui Nhon is a long way south of Hué and the dislocations of the war made it seem much further. As a true Buddhist and a dutiful mother, she went to try to gather together the various bits of her son (he had been blown apart by a mortar bomb), and convey them in a plastic bag to Hué for burial in a grave in the family plot near Nui Binh hill. The whole appalling episode was made even more horrific by the fact that however much she searched, Mme Bong was unable to find her son's left arm and so poor Van, according to Vietnamese Buddhist doctrine at least, is condemned to roam the earth inconsolably grieving for his missing limb.

Even so, still worse was yet to come.

At the beginning of the next year – 1968 – during the Tet (New Year) holidays, military catastrophe struck Hué. The North Vietnamese Army and the Viet Cong – lean, black-clothed, little men, toughened by years of warfare – suddenly surfaced from their guerrilla hideouts, invading part, or all, of a good many towns and cities in South Vietnam including the whole of Hué (which they occupied for a month) and even part of Saigon itself. They filled the streets of South Vietnam with bullets and bodies, and they filled the whole of South Vietnam with a sudden fear. Mme Bong's house in Hué – all the family had congregated there for the holidays – was actually occupied by communist soldiers who held them all hostage, and who also swiftly took over the citadel that dominates the city from the edge of the Perfume River, fortifying its ramparts against the inevitable American counter-attacks from the air and the desperate ground assault with tanks that finally ended the occupation. By the time the city was finally won back, the communists and the Americans between them had virtually destroyed this beautiful place.

I was not in Vietnam when the communist offensive began; as a respite from covering wars, I had been in America on a wholly different assignment. As a matter of fact, I had been interviewing Mae West at her home in Hollywood when suddenly one night every TV programme was interrupted to show horrific pictures of furious street fighting the length and breadth of South Vietnam – even in the capital, Saigon. It was particularly horrifying because there had been no warning. American Vietnam 'experts' had not predicted the likelihood of such a widespread communist uprising; they were baffled. So was everyone else. What could this mean? Was the war lost?

In retrospect, we know it did not win the war for the North outright. But it shook the Western world, particularly, of course, the Americans, from President Lyndon Johnson downwards.

Fresh from Mae West I returned to my hotel, shattered by what I had seen and heard, and desperately worried about Mme Bong's family in Hué. The city had been overrun. I was not surprised to receive an urgent telephone call from my news editor in London at five in the morning, telling me in no uncertain terms to stop having what he called 'a good time' in Los Angeles and get out to Vietnam as quick as I could.

Pausing only to phone Miss West to inform her that our talks must be suspended ('Let me know as soon as you're back,' Miss West's familiar growl came down the line, 'and we'll con-tinue'), I flew to San Francisco for a Vietnamese visa and then grabbed a seat on the first available Pan American flight to Bangkok. The plane had been chartered by the American army and was full of soldiers and their equipment being rushed out to stem the communist flood, and I was compelled to fly First Class to get on the plane at all (only years later did the management of my newspaper agree that I had spent the money wisely).

I reached Hué at last just as American army reinforcements were rushing to relieve the city. On the road from the airport (the one I had taken with Vua three years before) I felt at a total loss, experiencing a kind of nightmare, imagining I was one of General Patton's soldiers storming across France in a rush of vehicles and petrol tankers with the drivers' feet stamping on the gas. It was quite unreal: I came back to Hué in a truck loaded with GIs, cigarettes clamped between their teeth in unshaven jaws, guns at the ready, roaring and rattling across little bridges that had been blown up and hastily – and sometimes only partially – repaired, past other GIs crouching grimly in sandbagged strong points, while – adding to the deafening cacophony of the armoured vehicles – jets and helicopter gunships dived to bombard the green countryside around us with napalm and high explosives.

It was a scene of wild and frightening hysteria. I had taken the road from the airport to Hué many times before, but now it was like living a dream in which one turned a corner and found a familiar and well-loved scene had mysteriously undergone a hideous change, and I wondered fearfully what scenes I would find in the city itself. Our eardrums tortured by the shattering noise of aircraft and bursting explosives, our truck twisted and skidded on muddy roads between poor blasted houses whose missing walls had been shot out. Terrified Vietnamese – to me they looked horrifyingly like Mme Bong, Qué and Minh – refugees from the fighting, scurried along under bundles of possessions and were forced quaking into the roadside ditches to avoid the trucks. Everywhere I looked there were American and South Viet-namese soldiers. Sometimes I saw down side alleys armoured personnel carriers loaded with helmeted Americans in bulky flak jackets waiting like gangsters in ambush. This was not the Vietnam I had come to love.

Worst of all, ahead of us we could hear the terrible crunch of bombs relentlessly falling on Hué itself – on the residential area, on the market. We could see columns of smoke, and we could hear the sound of rockets roaring down presumably on to the citadel, from screaming planes that flashed like splinters of silver – ironically beautiful – in a platinum sky. But I wondered how many rockets or bombs would miss the citadel and fall on peaceful streets instead? On Mme Bong's house, for example?

Arriving near the banks of the Perfume River I jumped from the truck and stood for a moment petrified with horror at what I saw. The north bank, where Mme Bong's house stood, looked like the worst hit parts of London after a bad night of blitzing – surely the family couldn't have survived?

Chapter 3

I began to push my way through the horde of Vietnamese civilians who were milling across the one makeshift gangway over the river – the old girdered bridge had been dynamited by someone's sappers (the Viet Cong's, probably). At times I found myself calf-deep in the river water where the press of people had bent the thin planks dangerously low. But in the end, sweating and bedraggled, my trouser legs soaked, I reached the family's street, expecting to find it a blackened shambles of gutted houses. I thought bitterly, 'Well, that's the end of my Vietnamese family.'

'*My* Vietnamese family': that is exactly what passed through my mind. After only three years of fairly haphazard acquaintance with Mme Bong, Minh, Qué and their friends, in the heat, the hopeless confusion of the moment and in an apparent certainty of their total destruction, they did suddenly seem to have become 'mine'. The thought that they might have all been killed filled me with a sudden nausea that made it difficult even to go on walking. I imagined not live human beings, but a huddle of grey, drained corpses.

To my astonishment they were there after all, and alive. The market and teashops across the road in Tran Hung Dao Street had been devastated by the bombardment and the street itself was a shambles of broken glass and scorched beams. But there was Minh and one of his friends – Ngoc, I think – standing outside the untouched doorway of No. 103, first waving to me, astonished, then shouting and running through the rubble to meet me.

I had made up my mind they were all dead. But there they were: Minh in the lead, Ngoc, Qué and Vua a short way behind him, crunching as quickly as they could through the rubble as I started to run towards them. When we came close, Minh leapt into the air, as Vietnamese do at such times, landing with his arms round my neck and his legs grasping my waist. Then on his two feet again and babbling with excitement, he led me into the house that a few years earlier had become my home-from-home, into the familiar hallway that served both as a dining- and sitting-room where I had first met Mme Bong three years before. There she was now, pale and smiling, standing calmly in her white *ao dai*, among broken tiles, burned beams, bullet-pocked walls, as though nothing much had happened – as if the Viet Cong and North Vietnamese Army had passed by peacefully and had ignored, not occupied, her house for the last month.

I learned exactly what had happened at No. 103 during the communist occupation as soon as the rest of the family dried their eyes – when I reached the door they had been weeping, with shock and relief, I suppose.

It had been like this, they told me: the family had gathered as usual in the house for the Tet holiday – ten of them, uncles, aunts, cousins, sons, Qué and his parents, Ngoc and Tam and Vua (friends of Minh's), not to mention the short, stubby-legged dog, Mimi.

There was a small mortar crater in the floor in a corner, and, by chance, at the moment I saw it a sudden deafening explosion rocked the street, making me jump. The family laughed at me: they had got used to sudden bangs in the last few weeks; nothing could alarm them now.

Then Mme Bong began the story. 'When the first fusillades began – this was in the very early days of Tet – we had all been asleep,' she said. 'The Viet Cong were firing across the river at American headquarters – you know, at their compound. We thought it was like any other shooting and would soon stop, but when we all got up and came downstairs we saw the Viet Cong soldiers in the street outside. About twenty of them at first, then more – about sixty, I suppose. They wore shorts and khaki shirts and no caps. Young – seventeen or eighteen. They couldn't come into the houses in this street because by then everyone had barred the shutters.' Remembering all this she bent her head. 'But I knew we would suffer.'

Minh chipped in: 'A South Vietnamese soldier lay wounded and bleeding outside our door all the morning. Nobody dared to come out and help him. Then one of a Viet Cong patrol walked up and just shot him.' Minh's face puckered in disbelief as if he was going to cry. 'He was harmless,' he said, 'but he just shot him.'

One of Minh's cousins took up the story. 'Viet Cong soldiers soon came into the house and from the way they spoke we could tell that some of them were from this region. Some, though, were from the North, real Tonkinese. They scared us. Although they threatened us, they didn't harm us, actually. They only insisted they were winning the war and told us that therefore we should support them.'

Somebody else said, 'They sat about some of the time, singing communist songs. They gave us documents to study, all to do with their ideology. They wanted us to carry arms and ammunition for them, too.'

I asked, 'Did many Vietnamese from here help them with their arms-carrying and so on?'

'Only some people – trishaw drivers, people like that.'

'What did students like you think of them, Minh?'

'Well,' he replied, 'the Viet Cong told us they were fighting for the independence of Vietnam from the Americans. I don't like the Americans, as you know, but I don't like the communists either. I'm sure some students went with the Viet Cong, but, believe me, not many.'

*

35

So much for Saigon government accusations that the militant Buddhist Struggle Group students of Hué were fellow-travellers – or even active supporters of the Viet Cong, longing for a communist victory. They had evidently had every opportunity to throw in their lot with the communists in the last month, during Tet. They had chosen not to. It fitted everything I had heard Minh and his friends tell me many times in this very house.

Mme Bong added that she was chiefly concerned to get her male relatives, Minh and the rest, out of Hué now in case the Viet Cong returned and carried them off. 'You see, they took a lot of young men away with them by force,' she added. That alarmed me. I hadn't thought of the possibility that they might return.

'You know,' said Vua, rather surprisingly I thought, 'they seemed to think that because we were Buddhist students and had been in the struggle movement we would welcome them.'

I supposed they would have thought that; after all, that was precisely what the Americans had thought. Both Minh and Vua had actually taken carbines down to Danang and had manned barricades against troops Thieu had had flown up there by American pilots in American planes.

Both sides – North and South – must have been surprised by the reaction of the young Buddhists of Hué to the communist occupation of their city. I imagine the communists were particularly mortified by the failure of the young people of Hué to welcome them – or willingly to go away with them. In one part of the city, someone in the room added, hundreds of Vietnamese civilians were led off, presumably to be executed, with bandaged eyes and their hands tied behind their backs. Many more were forced to act as coolies, he said, and to carry Viet Cong wounded up into the hills of northwest Annam during the fighting. Marching fifty kilometres or so, without food and water; four men to each wounded man; at night because the communists said it was necessary to pass through villages before dawn to avoid the American flares and patrolling helicopters. It was surprising, he added, how little medicine the communists seemed to have. They didn't seem to know the way very well either.

I learned something of that harsh time from Bao Ninh's *The Sorrow of War*.

Bao Ninh's testament to the war in Vietnam was first published in 1991 in Hanoi and won a literary prize there. He was born in Hanoi in 1952. He served in the Vietnam war, fighting for the North against the Americans for six years from 1969 and was one of only ten who survived that holocaust out of five hundred who went with him. *The Sorrow of War* was translated into English and French and was compared – rightly – by Western reviewers to *All Quiet on the Western Front*, Mailer's *The Naked and the Dead* and the poems of Wilfred Owen.

The novel set out in horrific detail the fears and agonies experienced by North Vietnamese conscripts fighting in the jungles and mountains of Vietnam. Apart from the prize in Hanoi, it became a bestseller in Vietnam, but the communist authorities in Hanoi must have taken another look at it and found, I suppose, that it was *too* honest and too revealing. It set out in depth, as I have said, the agonized feelings of a sensitive young North Vietnamese fighting the American tanks, planes and helicopters in many bloody battles over that long period. But what was worse from Hanoi's point of view was that it also gave the game away, so to speak, about the propaganda deceptions foisted by communist cadres on war-weary ex-conscripts concerning such things as the allegedly pathetic war efforts of the Southern soldiers who, after all, badly led though they were, still acquitted themselves heroically from time to time. It is worth remembering that the Southern soldiers were more or less the same sort of poor Vietnamese peasants who formed the majority of the soldiers of the communist North.

Anyway, Bao Ninh and his book are now in limbo. Bao Ninh was not a peasant. His fascinating novel was unique: a model of honest, no-holds-barred writing, including a calm and sad appraisal of the dreadful fighting of that time.

'The two weeks of retreat after the Tet offensive in 1968,' he writes, 'was an unfortunate time for them [the Northern soldiers], carrying the wounded and dragging their feet through the jungle, while overhead were the spotter planes and bombers.'

American troops were all around and in less than a fortnight Bao Ninh's scouts had been encircled twice, and twice, in utter desperation, had broken out of the traps, fighting fearlessly. Some units, he says, were in total disarray and badly beaten up.

A young man at Mme Bong's I had never seen before but who had obviously been on one of these enforced evacuations of the wounded guerrillas said, 'Where I was there were lots of Viet Cong soldiers coming and going. When we got to a rough shelter on a hill we were made to sign a paper saying that we had delivered so many wounded for the soldiers of the National Liberation Front. They got very angry if anyone referred to them as Viet Minh or Viet Cong. They shot one man I knew for saying "Viet Minh". Then they asked us to stay with them, saying they had won in Hué and everywhere else, too, and that now was the time to make a choice. But we said we would rather go home. And we went all alone back through the dark.'

At this point two things startled us all. First, after I, moved by what I'd heard, had whispered, 'What a catastrophe for you', Minh all of a sudden had a sort of breakdown. He leant forward intently and shouted, 'Not a catastrophe, no! It's war, and this is normal! So? Well, we must have peace, mustn't we? Oh yes, yes, yes!' His voice rose in a hysterical crescendo, in so uncharacteristic a way that it shook me. It was unlike any Vietnamese exhibition of anguish I had ever witnessed before.

Almost at once, as if in response to Minh's wild shout, the second shock came. A violent explosion suddenly rocked the already weakened structure of the building, and a shower of loose stones fell into the room. (Later I discovered two Viet Cong mortar shells had hit an American ammunition ship. It had blown up about 600 yards away.)

In a while, I went out to take a look at the damage to other houses behind Mme Bong's. Here I got another shock. The residential and commercial area of Hué resembled something out of Goya. Whole streets were laid waste. Rubble choked the sidewalks, there were bomb craters in the tarmac and the blackened shells of burned-out cars. A truck was embedded in a wall. The Americans had dropped huge bombs here on what they imagined was the citadel – 750- and 500-pounders. Where they actually fell was one of the more fearfully damaged parts of a hideously shattered city. This was a residential area; it had been packed with families like Mme Bong's gathering for the Tet holiday. Now you had to walk about it with a handkerchief to your nose. You expected to see rats. Shops were in ruins, like the houses. I saw crowds scrabbling and clawing at the grilles of stores where a few sacks of rice were being handed out. The lucky ones – paying four times the normal price – quickly loaded the sacks on to bicycles and scurried away. They looked, supposing one approached too close, as if they would turn and defend the rice like famished dogs with a bone.

A Vietnamese bystander who spoke good French told me as he pointed to a monstrous pile of rubble, 'The man who lived there was shot by the Viet Cong. Now his house is destroyed by the Americans. Curious, eh?'

He stopped, trembling, before another pile. There were plenty to choose from. 'There are thirty people under this one, can you believe it?' Vietnamese were hard at it, digging into another mound of bricks and earth. 'They are still bringing the bodies out of there,' the man said. 'Two families, about twenty people, eight survivors so far.'

So my tour went on. The stench of the dead was overpowering. In an open space between the houses mutilated corpses were being wrapped in sheets. Three men in makeshift nose-masks dug graves. Women and children stood around keening and shaking with sobs. A woman, beside herself with grief, flung herself on a freshly dug mound of earth, rolling on it, hammering it with her fists.

We went on down street after street – or rather, the wrecks of streets – stepping through fragments of glass, pathetic muddied wrappings of Tet holiday gifts, filth and dead rats, until we came to the great ornamental gate of the citadel which had just been stormed by the US Marines. The citadel's solid walls were punctured by shells, sliced by flying metal, and the gateway itself was riddled by everything from bullets to rockets. Inside the citadel, in its large grassy interior, there seemed to be no shop, house or royal divan that was not wholly or partially destroyed. The Americans had used tanks here after the air strikes, and the Viet Cong and North Vietnamese had fired back with rockets and heavy machine-guns from the camouflaged foxholes you saw everywhere. No wonder it was such a mess.

It is so unreal, I kept thinking. That day Hué was no more the city I had known and loved than a friend lying in a street, charred and ripped by a bomb, is the human being one had once talked or made love to. As I said later in the dispatch I sent to my newspaper, 'Now, between them, General Giap and the US High Command have killed the flower of Vietnamese cities. You can disguise it in whatever military terms you like but in Hué a murder has been arranged.'

I believed every word I wrote.

Of course, my friends were extraordinarily lucky. No one knew then how many civilians were killed by one side or the other; perhaps they don't know even now. There were thought to be 3,000 government employees buried in two mass graves. While I was actually there I had heard that in a quarter of Hué, inhabited largely by army officers and civil servants, they were digging up the bodies of officials' relatives – men, women and children – who had had their hands tied behind their backs, had been led away, and then had been shot by the Viet Cong. Mothers stood about weeping, I was told, as the diggers worked, rushing forward to try to recognize relatives as the bodies were taken from the earth. This was in the garden of a secondary school: Gia Hoi school, on an island to the southeast of the city, used by the communists during the fighting as a command post. Among the dead were said to be a French priest and two German doctors.

This was one result of the human disaster brought on by the war. There was another. Near Hué's stadium I saw the American dead being brought in, wrapped in green plastic shrouds. They were loaded on to helicopters. I saw a growing pile of American uniforms, water bottles, rifles, and pathetic letters, one of which I read, ending, 'With love, and try and write soon, Mom'. Over my head American jets screeched down, raining napalm and rockets into trees a few hundred yards away, vaporizing them. It was all quite pointless. The damage had been done. Military casualties were heavy and rising. Most American civilians in the northern regions of South Vietnam would work from now on in a cloud of foreboding. Pacification and carefully built-up development programmes would certainly be in ruins, at least for the foreseeable future.

To me, the murder of Hué symbolized the entire war. The people had been raped – this is what I told myself as I turned wearily back towards Mme Bong's house – by two forces which they had come to distrust and fear. The Americans had regained Hué at the cost of destroying it; General Giap's communist forces thought they could win over people they wrongly considered ripe for conversion simply because they had opposed the Saigon government and the American presence. The communists, too – with the Americans – had to learn that there were three political forces in Vietnam, not two, and that the third one, the one that rejected the big-stick images of both Hanoi and Saigon, was very large and, when opportunity arose, courageous.

Standing in the stench of Hué's streets, I saw at least one thing very clearly: a criminal act had been committed here during Tet. Hué had become the prey of cynical ideologues who talked with unctuous arrogance of nationalism, communism or democracy and who, in the name of all these things, had destroyed it. Had destroyed it for no purpose, for no visible gain whatsoever.

That evening – an evening I shall never forget – Mme Bong said to me: 'You know, during the bombardment I sat thinking, "Suppose President Ho Chi Minh and President Johnson visited Hué at the same time and saw all this, and they said to each other: 'Why are we doing this?' and shook hands."' She looked at me quickly and added shyly: 'You think that's very stupid. Of course, I am not serious. It was only my dream.'

I put this into the piece to my newspaper, too. Mme Bong was not being stupid at all. I think she was absolutely right.

I took a plane back to Saigon as soon as I could to write my account of the disaster in Hué for my newspaper.

I had already made up my mind to end the piece with Mme Bong's remarks about the two presidents, Ho Chi Minh and Lyndon Johnson, visiting Hué and shaking hands. And as soon as possible I sat down at a typewriter in a room in the Caravelle Hotel and wrote about the appalling scenes I had witnessed. The only thing of major interest I find I had left out of it was any eyewitness account of the massacre by the communists of hundreds of civilian men, women and children, and their burial in a mass grave in the grounds of a secondary school on an island called Gia Hoi. I think I left it out because I was not absolutely sure it had actually occurred. Everything else I had been able to check for myself with my own eyes and ears. I had been horrified by what I had seen and heard, from the accounts of Minh and the others to the remark of the furious American colonel I had found preparing heavy mortars to bombard the residential part of the city who said to me (apropos the news reports that came daily in English and Vietnamese from London), 'You know what BBC stands for? British Communist Broadcasting Company, that's what.'

When the long piece had been written and typed out for the telex operator, I sent it to London. When it had gone, I collapsed into a chair in the hotel room, and let the tears fall. I thanked God I had visited Hué in 1965. I thanked God for Mme Bong and her family who had taught me something of Vietnamese life and thought . . .

As I do now.

Perhaps it will come as an anticlimax – or simply light relief – but I must add that when I returned to America from Vietnam after the tragedy of Hué I hastened to call Miss West, to see if we could carry on with our talks where they had been so brutally interrupted.

'Welcome back,' she breathed down the telephone. 'Ah thought you'd never come. We-e-ll, have a large drink to for-tifah yourself and then hurry on down here.' I needed no other urging.

For the next two days we discussed her life story upside down and inside out, as they say. We talked about her impending return to the silver screen in a film of Gore Vidal's *Myra Breckinridge*. And then, finally, I had to go. On the white landing outside her white front door, she put a restraining hand on my arm. She had something urgent she wanted to communicate, I could see that.

At last she murmured, 'Say, it *was* Veetnam you were in? You know, I used to know someone very, *very* important there.'

'You did, Miss West? Who was it? General Westmoreland?'

'No, no,' she said, impatiently.

'Ambassador Henry Cabot Lodge?'

'No, no, no!' She was becoming more irritated by the second.

She twisted her face up at me (she was very short despite her beehive hairdo, and I towered above her) and tried very hard to recall the name for probably the last time. 'His name was – uh, let's see – Ho . . . Ho . . . Ho . . . something.'

I couldn't believe it. 'Not Ho Chi Minh, Miss West? Not Ho Chi Minh?'

She was annoyed by my evident astonishment. 'Well, you'd better believe it, Mr Young. I *never* lie. It was in the nineteen-twenties. Maybe before you were born. In London. I had a show I wrote myself called just *Sex*. You know, spelled S-E-X. You can check that. And I was staying at the Carlton Hotel. There was this waiter, cook, I don't know what he was. I know he had the slinkiest eyes, though. We met in the corridor. We-ell . . .' She left things there. Her voice trailed off in a husky sigh, and she looked up at me from under her golden hairdo, seventy-something years old, with a tiny smile on her lips and the sauciest air imaginable.

Well, Miss West is dead now. And so is Ho Chi Minh. There is nobody alive to confirm or deny the story. So I will probably never know whether or not Mae West was having me on or actually did have a passing dalliance with Uncle Ho.

The trouble is that Ho Chi Minh *did* work at the Carlton Hotel in the Haymarket in London at some time around then. Mae West *did* write and stage her show *Sex* at about the same time – and in the Haymarket. Did they meet? It's possible, I suppose. But I really have no idea. All I know is what Mae West told me at the door of her apartment in West Hollywood.

Chapter 4

Mme Bong's troubles were not to end there. They began to seriously plague her almost as soon as I entered the doorway of 103 Tran Hung Dao Street. That was pure chance. Of course, they went back a good deal further than the day of my arrival; after all, she had lost her twenty-seven-year-old husband long before my first visit to Hué – during the French war against the Viet Minh. Why should they have ended when I left Hué to go back to talk show business with Mae West?

Even later – I mean, after the Tet tragedy I have just described – there was worse to come: Mme Bong's remaining son's capture by the communists, for example, and his imprisonment for seven years and his final exile in America. After all that time in prison – despite it, rather – he found there was to be no work for him in Vietnam; the trouble was he had never been a member of the Viet Cong or a soldier in the North Vietnamese Army.

But that is to jump ahead. For now, I will try to recall the first time I met Mme Bong and her family. It was very early in my time in Vietnam. I had arrived in Saigon in early 1965, just before the American Marines landed in Danang – 'stormed ashore' I should say (the Marines always 'storm ashore') – on this occasion into the arms, as it were, of a considerable number of smiling American newspapermen and photographers waiting for them on the beach itself. Of course, they landed unopposed – and now I wonder if those poor young men wading ashore through a light surf thought, when they saw the media 'welcoming committee', that it was going to be roses, roses all the way from then on.

Who knows what they thought? I, at any rate, was thinking what a beautiful country I had arrived in. I remember being in Saigon; taking the lift one evening soon after my arrival to the rooftop restaurant of the Caravelle Hotel, where I was staying. It was at the top of this quite high building and from it one had an excellent panoramic view – for Saigon was not a city of skyscrapers then. I could look out at both the countryside and the meandering river. Far away, the flash of artillery fire travelled round the horizon like summer lightning, and below me, on the city side, the drivers of the cyclos (the cycle rickshaws) in their mollusc hats pedalled their clients up and down the bar-lined street of Tu Do.

Across the square, lining its west side like the side of the 1930s transatlantic liner, was the Continental Hotel, its ground floor terrace packed with people – some Vietnamese in suits and ties, a few American officers – 'advisers', perhaps – a rowdy group of happy middle-aged journalists fresh from a military operation in the Delta and glad to have survived it. For some reason the terrace, though it was exposed to the street, was thought to be terrorist-proof – I could never understand why.

Looking back at the wide, muddy river from the Caravelle's restaurant I was surprised to see that a ship – I suppose really only its masts and its upper structure, including its bridge – I had seen on my right had suddenly appeared behind me. I had to turn my head to find it. It had to do with the zigzag contortions of the river, of course; but after all these years I have never forgotten that ship of unknown nationality weaving its way up the Saigon River. I still remember the thrill that possessed me then at the thought of being in Indochina. Of course, I had no idea then that I would be here for nine years off and on.

That was at the beginning, before I thought I saw the unsure, anxious peoples of the earth – the French and the Americans in this case –

impelled by their own miseries and insecurities to desolate the relatively poor but happy peoples. It was a vision that started to grow clearer as the years went by.

Every afternoon at about five o'clock journalists gathered in a briefing-room in the Rex (it had been an hotel once, and now was the place where American public relations officials gave the press daily figures based on official reports of action in the countryside). The press briefings were known, for obvious reasons, to journalists as the 'Five O'Clock Follies'. I have come upon some haphazard notes of briefings I attended in late 1965. Here they are in their rough state:

> No major VC attacks last week. 640 lost ARVN [South Vietnam-ese Army] and 168 US (killed) 100 captured.

> 'Operation Starlight' near Chu Lai. VC defections and losses: VC 614 killed (body count); 109 weapons captured.

> SV [South Vietnamese] intelligence unearthed: training, recruiting area; elements of VC regiment. No heavy weapons taken. [Where was this? I wonder now.]

> 1 Oct 1965:
> Biggest operation in the Delta for months.

> 5 Battalions and air support. 68 VC killed; 6 captured (body count). Perhaps another 100 VCs KIA [killed in action] or wounded.

> One VC assault craft ambushed on river and sunk: sub-machine-guns captured.

On another page, I found a kind of order of battle which I can only suppose represented the composition of forces involved against the communists near Saigon.

NZ artillery [there was always a battery of heavy guns manned by New Zealanders in South Vietnam].

4 SV Para Bns

1 Australian Bn [there was usually a fine battalion of Australian volunteers, about the best trained and most reliable soldiers in Vietnam. They were withdrawn by an incoming Prime Minister, Gough Whitlam, in about 1972].

2 US Bns

2 Ranger Bns [South Vietnamese].

From the number of troops involved it must have been a considerable operation. I have forgotten what it achieved, if anything.

Next, an assessment of the military situation made pretty gloomy reading.

2 more months rain in the north. Rain helps the VC. Thus there may be strong attacks on ARVN.

– outlying provinces still not cleared (low priority) and there are still problems there.

– B-52s [American heavy bombers] used because they don't disrupt in-country forces.

– frequent sweeps keep VC moving, denying them time to regroup, train and collect supplies; and aiming to drive VC into the hills and the jungle where they could be plagued by malaria.

– *Delta*: villages cleared, but villagers have to have confidence that the security forces will arrive if VC attack.

– air artillery has tipped the balance – and the VC are paying the price for classic ambushes.

And so my ragged notes go on. The briefings continued throughout the war – until the North Vietnamese Army entered Saigon in 1975, I suppose. One entry I find particularly interesting: a few scribbled notes on South Vietnamese reactions to the American military build-up in the country which started in 1965:

It has bred a sense of failure. S Viets worry that American bombs will fall on them. That they will cause more and more refugees. That the feelings of 'Oh, all right. Let the Americans do everything' will increase. That there will be more incidents of sabotage.

The boisterous American presence hid Vietnam like a crude curtain. The true Vietnam slid by unnoticed if one was not careful: but the movement and colour of this gorgeous country remained – the pageant of birds in the morning, the black-pyjamaed stooping bodies in their conical hats rising and falling in the paddy fields, the butterscotch-skinned boys diving among the water-buffaloes into the waterways of the Delta.

Even in Saigon, the cheerful grinning faces that surrounded one in the street belied the horrors that lay on the outskirts of the city – the crash of bombs and exploding shells, the delayed scream of jet engines that had already passed overhead, the clank-clank of the ubiquitous helicopters. The Vietnamese were jolly; tricky, it is true: quicksilver, I called them. They were sentimental, nature-loving, loving the landscape they inhabited; and sensuous as well so that they loved the feel of a friend's hand in theirs.

Long before I arrived there people had told me of the beauties of the Vietnamese countryside; I had heard from someone, in particular, of the glorious imperial capital of Annam in the centre of the country, the city of Hué on the Perfume River. I can't remember now who it was – certainly not a colleague because most journalists didn't go far from Saigon or the military units in the field, and not many journalists had set foot in Hué as far as I knew. The last emperor, Bao Dai, was in exile on the French Riviera, but few missed the decadent ruler whom the French had liked and used but who had ruled with an arrogance befitting an ancient mandarin. Hué, it was said, was as self-consciously beautiful as ever.

At any rate, I soon found myself seated in a DC-6 of Air Vietnam flying on my way from Tan San Nhat airport in Saigon to Phu Bai, the tiny airstrip that served Hué. I remember dimly wondering how old the propeller-driven aircraft could be as I listened to the deafening whirr of its four engines and felt the sudden dips and shudders as we drove into clouds as thick as cottonwool.

I wondered if my next-door neighbour, a Vietnamese, was going to be sick on my shoes – he looked pale enough and occasionally his face twitched as though he was feeling desperate. He looked too young to have flown very often and that might, I thought, account for his evident queasiness. It *was* rather bumpy.

It turned out I was quite mistaken. For it was Vua sitting on my right-hand side, Vua whose natural twitch became very familiar to me in the years that followed, though it is less so now that he has moved to a town somewhere in far-away Texas.

'You are American?' he shouted above the roar of the engines. No, I told him, English. An English journalist going to have a look at the capital of Annam. I added that I had heard it was very beautiful.

He was pleased at that.

'*Vous avez beaucoup d'amis à Hué?*' he asked.

'I know no one there at all,' I replied.

'If you like I can meet you tomorrow outside the cinema across the river. The cinema: I'll show you where it is exactly.'

I saw the city for the first time in a sort of haze of excitement. First of all – arriving by taxi from the airport at Phu Bai, which is some miles away – I immediately recognized the Perfume River. The river divided the little city more or less in two; curving to the south under the bridge, it dived into the heart of the residential quarter, and disappeared, I suppose, to the sea. More important, swinging past the citadel and what looked like the major part of Hué – it turned out that Mme Bong's house faced on to the river – it continued inland and northwards, past Vua's little house, which had a garden like a small apron that ran down to the water, past the pagoda with the seven tiers, and wavered on towards the foothills, which accompanied the smooth silvery water that ran between gentle banks of vivid green with frequent copses of bushy trees and tall stands of bamboo – until the hills became huge blue-grey ramparts against the sky and the river vanished among them. I was to learn during quiet nights on the river with the Bong family, in sampans, eating food we had brought with us and with Vua playing the guitar, that those ramparts were constantly illuminated by flashes of gunfire somewhere to the northwest. And sometimes, when fighting was heavy, the flashes ran round the horizon as I had seen them do in Saigon. And sometimes a deep, long rumble ran through those suddenly sinister hills to remind us that life here was not, after all, a picnic.

Vua did show me where the cinema was, and I arranged to meet him there next morning at nine o'clock. Bang on time, he was waiting for me by the cinema with a friend – a short, thick-set Vietnamese of about his age.

'C'est mon ami,' explained Vua. 'Il s'appelle Minh.'

'My mother's house is just down the road,' said Minh. 'She would like to meet you.'

So that was how it happened. I have known Mme Bong for more than thirty years now. And of course Minh, her son, who now ekes out a living in Virginia, USA.

*

Time passed.

After a year or two, Minh went to the cadet school at Tu Duc and I went there to visit him. It was family day, I think. At any rate, cadets in fatigues were vociferously greeting friends and parents and, surprisingly, a few couples lay around on the grass with their arms around each other. Small boys in shorts and sandals had set up Coca-Cola stalls. In intense heat, Tu Duc was evidently *en fête*.

Minh had said: 'Don't bring food. It all has to be eaten the same day, and then they come and clear it away. A little fruit at the most, please. But it isn't worth bothering about. Books? I've no time for reading here.'

He looked fresh and well, and he was beginning to grow up; small thin hairs sprouted on his upper lip. Minh was stocky even then, almost plump. But the 'little warlord' look I used to laugh about with Vua had gone. He would be here for ten months, he told me. Then he would be released into government administration.

More incidents from the past come illuminated irregularly by flashes of lightning, accompanied, it seemed, more and more by sinister rolls of thunder like the sound of the guns that seemed to be growing louder in the hills around us.

In a letter in French from Minh in, I suppose, 1972, he wrote:

We must write often because we are so far away from one another . . . I will enrol in the administration school, but a few months later I have to go back to the army. It is obligatory. Qué, too, has had to join the infantry. Vua is leaving the Agricultural College [I think it was in Quang Ngai] *as an agricultural engineer.*

Later, Minh wrote again:

Both Qué and I are in parts of the army where we do not go to combat. So we are not forced to kill anyone – and that gives us great joy. After all, we are in the army only as an obligatory service, so we are both lucky. Vua is luckier still; he is near Qui Nhon working on an agricultural training project . . . He too is killing no one. And like us, he has no desire to. Perhaps, my dear brother, we are really the most lucky ones in this war – which, as you know well, we did not desire and want to end – because we are not obliged to bomb our own people.

In this I heard pathetic echoes of the Buddhist Struggle Group philosophy. Why, oh why, (I thought) hadn't the Americans' favourite Vietnamese generals paid serious attention to Thich Tri Quang? Mightn't the war be over by now – or at least in a state of peaceful negotiation?

It was at about this time that Mme Bong wrote me a heartbreaking letter that displayed such a contrast with her habitual sang-froid that I was seriously worried:

Cher Monsieur [that is how she always addressed me and she continues to do so to this day],

Minh, my only son, and Qué are now both back in the army. It is a bad time. Alas, my only surviving son has left home. I am alone with my daughter and my little grandchild. It is so lonely. If my dear son is killed, I don't know what I should do. We think now this terrible war will never end. It is a kind of life for us now. My poor country. My poor children.

It is a kind of life for us now, she had said, meaning the war. Of course, it would be after thirty years or so. Reading her letter,

I remembered something Vua's brother, an army doctor at a camp near Phu Bai airport called Ut, had said to me. I had noted it down. 'I hope in the near future when you will be here, the situation will be better and you will not work any more as a reporter but come as a traveller.'

The near future? It has taken almost a quarter of a century for that to come about, and now Ut is living in exile with Vua in Texas.

Sometimes, naturally, the lightning-flashes reveal a good time in the grim retrospect. For example, Vua's wedding party in his family's little house between the Perfume River and the track that leads to the seven-storey pagoda. It was a sweltering day and Vua and his friends (including Minh) and relatives sweated under their long Vietnamese silk shifts and round hats. Despite the heat, everybody got a bit tipsy. I see in my mind's eye a man putting his head back in a sort of drunken ecstasy and closing his eyes and singing a song in Vietnamese. He picked his teeth with a matchstick and I was suddenly afraid that in his tipsiness he would swallow it. Vua's uncle poured brandy in his glass. '*Encore une goutte ou deux*,' he giggled. '*Encore une goutte*.' He began to recite poetry in French, sometimes forgetting the end of the line. 'The mountains bend down to the Hué – no, no – to the river . . . ah, yes – the river. That's better . . .' He giggled again and everybody laughed with him happily.

The tables were covered with a mass of little plates of food too hot to eat, and the plates were placed on banana or coconut leaves. On the river people passing the house and seeing the party stood up in their motor boats and waved and cheered. Minh's face under his silk round Annamese hat was bright red. He had been at the brandy, too.

1972 was the year in which one of Qué's two brothers was killed in action, near Qui Nhon. Qué was as quiet as usual when the news came. No tears were shed, nothing said. The brother's body was not recovered, although Mme Bong and Qué's old father went down there to look for it. The fire-fight was too heavy and lasted too long.

It was about this time that I found Qué, on leave in Hué, reading Camus's *Le Mythe de Sisyphe*, and from it he quoted to me those two sentences which have haunted me since.

'I shall remember that until I die,' Qué told me, with a quiet gentle smile without which he would have been almost ugly. Qué had a long lugubrious face and when he smiled that wide, gentle smile, he reminded me of Dickens's Smike. Even in those days he had the habit of long silences and of staring into space.

We hardly ever talked of the war, but once I see from my notes he said to me: 'The argument against communism must be material or moral, mustn't it, Gavin? But the conditions we find here now are unemployment, rising prices, and corruption, *n'est-ce pas*? So no moral or material argument exists; there is no real patriotism in Saigon, I mean. So how can we resist? And yet we want to resist – most of us, you know – and we cannot. Isn't that the tragedy of it, Gavin?'

All the time, his white-haired father sat at the door quietly rolling his cigarettes, while his mother served rice wine, cheap and fiery, to cyclo drivers. They were as poor as church mice – as anything you can imagine.

After a few weeks, Qué was given the job of counting the expenditure of shells in some South Vietnamese army artillery base in Danang. At least, as Minh had written, Qué was not killing anyone. I doubted whether he could even accurately tot up the number of shells in his armoury or whatever it was. He certainly hadn't got that sort of mathematical mind.

In 1972 there was the great offensive towards Hué by the North Vietnamese Army. It was wonderfully successful, and the worst thing that could have happened to the South seemed about to happen: the fall of Hué. The once glorious capital of Annam, the jewel of central Vietnam, appeared ready to fall to the communists. I reported to my newspaper my doleful assessment that if the northernmost provincial capitals of Quang Tri and Hué fell, they would have gone for good and would inevitably be communized by force. The terrain, as far as I could see, ruled against the recapture of those two cities. To the North lay the DMZ (the Demilitarized Zone) that separated, at least on paper, the two warring parts of Vietnam. To the West were the convenient and attack-proof mountains that slopped over into Laos and enfolded the mysterious tentacles of the Ho Chi Minh trail, mountains that now seemed to lean over and threaten me. And to the South, a huge mountain ridge blocked the way to Danang, the last great American airbase.

Even Western military experts in Saigon had told me, 'Hué, now. That's different. That's a *major* prize. The North could negotiate with Hué.'

When I heard about the communist advances in the north and the rout of the South Vietnamese Army units there, I hurried back to Hué. Not that I wanted to see it in ruins and under occupation once more. Far from it. I had had enough of that kind of horror in 1968. But of course I had to see how Mme Bong and those of her family who remained in Hué were faring and, as Graham Greene put it in *The Quiet American*, 'if one writes about war, self-respect demands that occasionally one shares the risks.'

From the airstrip at Phu Bai, I pushed up by ramshackle taxi beyond Hué towards the DMZ, the invisible border between the North and the South. Quang Tri had been levelled by one side or the other – it was nothing but a dimly smoking mass of ruins and ashes. So was Dong Ha, an unappealing little town at the best of times, which I had last seen when Minh was briefly posted there as something called Assistant Administrative Officer. I heard there that the South Vietnamese commanders in the North had been dismissed for incompetence, although I was never to hear any confirmation of that report.

I stood on the road running north–south from the DMZ to Hué

and wondered if this was the end of everything. I felt a sudden wild rage against those responsible for military calamities like this.

Who in God's name *was* responsible? Who the hell is to blame, I silently raged, standing on the Street Without Joy as the French had named it, sweating in a combination of the heat and stark fear, as South Vietnamese troops swarmed past me – panicked, fleeing, striving to escape south, to the next big city, which was Hué. Why not blame the American advisers and their boss, General Abrams? How the devil had they and he failed to predict the inability of American shelling and airpower to halt a conventional North Vietnamese advance down a flat coastal plain without benefit of air cover? It seemed that a fairly new military truth – well, no: on second thoughts, a fairly old one – was about to be born. This was that bombs and shells cannot halt a determined offensive without adequate ground forces acting aggressively in cooperation with the gunners and the airmen.

Maybe that was known before all this happened, I thought, in which case, how could one account for the manifest optimism in high American military and ambassadorial quarters in Saigon since the offensive began? I bitterly recalled that an old official named Elsworth Bunker, the American ambassador in Saigon for the last five years, had announced a month before that the offensive would run out of steam after six or seven weeks. That meant it should collapse about next week. Yet, as I could see, the Northerners were still steaming ahead. Once again the cause almost certainly was over-optimistic reports written by ignorant field officers – or *maybe* (I was prepared to believe anything now, although I didn't report it) by corrupt field officers, busily fudging reports to boost their careers and to bamboozle senior American staff officers in Saigon and, by extension, in Washington, D.C.

The trouble with this was that sooner rather than later they would be found out – but too late to save Mme Bong and her children from fates that very likely might be worse than death.

With a certain difficulty – it is difficult to make haste when all the world around you seems to be panicking down the very road you want to take – I made my way back to Hué, and headed towards No. 103. The Bong house was deserted. The family and their friends had gone from Hué. The only people at the door were a few drunken cyclo drivers, who yelled Vietnamese obscenities at me and began to look very threatening.

'I would leave, *monsieur*,' a man I had never seen before whispered in my ear. 'You can do nothing here.' He was right. I turned away, desperate, unarmed, feeling abandoned.

Down the street the market was in flames. Vietnamese deserters had set it ablaze. I could see them throwing away their uniforms in the street, cavorting about in nothing but their cotton shorts. It certainly looked a good time to go. In another minute one of them would see me and then God knew what they would do. They were delirious with the cheap hooch they had drunk and the guilt of desertion and defeat. Dancing in the light of those flames they looked like a half-naked gang of howling devils.

I made my way back alone across the darkened bridge to the other side of the Perfume River, wondering how one could forget how much a habit Vietnam had become. I had forgotten how accustomed one was to the casual gunfire – the crack and thump of machine-guns and rifles and the roar of rockets and the even louder, ear-splitting roar of jet bombers diving overhead. On the road outside Quang Tri it was not the sound of guns that had alarmed me; what had filled me with acute fear was the sense of a catastrophic defeat and the sight of the rout, the naked panic of the fleeing soldiers.

I had never seen Hué like this. I had seen it full of communist soldiers, and I had seen bodies galore in the streets. I had never before seen it full of drunken men shamelessly shedding their arms and uniforms; I had never before been on the point of being assaulted at the door of Mme Bong's house. That suddenly made me terribly aware that I was an alien to the Vietnamese – possibly a hated American – at any rate, different and very, very vulnerable.

The Bong family had never been away before, not even in Tet in 1968. This time they must have sensed something evil in the wind. I now know that Mme Bong had moved to Nha Trang for a time, partly to avoid the trouble she felt was brewing in Hué, partly to visit her new son-in-law, Ho Trang, who had become a district chief somewhere near that seaside city. One of her two daughters had fairly recently married him, and already a second baby was due.

I went to the only modern hotel Hué possessed at that time – an austere building I had never visited before on the other bank of the river, facing the burning marketplace. I got a room at the back, away from the side exposed to the river, and prepared to pass what turned out to be one of the most terrifying nights of my life. Everyone I had asked for an opinion – an American I met (heading for the army compound where, I knew, they only gave shelter to other Americans), Vietnamese met casually on the road, and still others standing idly at the hotel's reception desk – all of them predicted that the communists could enter the city that night, or at least very soon.

'They all around,' a young male receptionist at the hotel told me, grinning as if he, too, were a communist member of the Viet Cong. (Perhaps he was; who knew?)

I went to my room early. I had a bottle of Red Label whisky in my bag; I would need it, as my thoughts roved wildly over the hideous possibilities. Suppose the communists came in again? They stayed a month last time. Several foreigners had been killed in cold blood. Now and then explosions nearby made the hotel shake. I heard shouts and stray cries in the night that could be challenges. Curfew came at eleven o'clock and my apprehension set in. Shots rang out near the hotel – on the river side or mine, I couldn't tell. I began on the Scotch and to make feeble, desperate plans, having minimal faith in any of them.

Suppose the Viet Cong came in to the hotel and started to search the rooms. Mine was on the first floor; it wouldn't take them long to reach me.

I seriously wondered if the ledge above the only cupboard would conceal me, and for how long. What would I eat there; just as important, how could I pee? The whisky went down my throat, and the shots rang out again and again. Single shots; but who would have fired them? Once a burst of firing made me think that a Viet Cong patrol had landed on the river bank under the hotel. I heard footsteps pounding along the corridor and all of a sudden fists beat wildly on my door. *They were here!* I froze, but no one came in and soon, thanks to the whisky, I wouldn't care what happened, and I took another swig.

The hotel seemed empty and infinitely vulnerable. I was, as Greene had felt in the Delta, 'fear taken neat'. In my desperation I thought of Mme Bong – of how she would laugh at me; I thought of how she had laughed the time the sudden big bang had made me jump in her house. I thought of my colleagues in Saigon or far away in the safety of Hong Kong or Singapore. How I would make them roar with laughter when I told them about this evening. The only trouble was I wouldn't be alive to tell them. That I knew for a certainty. It was the reason I was so glad of the whisky. I am a fair whisky drinker but I always make a habit of drowning it in water and adding lots of ice. I was certainly not accustomed to this – the neat stuff drunk straight out of the bottle.

Nevertheless the whisky in the end had the desired effect. Thankfully, I slept. And waking to find the sun streaming in, I felt my face bristly with not shaving, and a mouth, as a British marine once described it in my hearing, like a zoo-keeper's boots. When I staggered downstairs I found the ugly young receptionist eyeing me with an expression of profound distaste.

'So they no come?' he said with an evil smile.

'I don't think so,' I managed to reply, my head throbbing, my tongue like flannel. 'Unless you are one of them.'

He smiled his sinister smile. 'Who knows?'

About a year later – but to me it might have been a decade – better times resumed in what seemed another world. There was a ceasefire in 1973, and so Mme Bong returned to her house in Hué. The walls there had become three-ply now, and the roof was made of sheet-iron which replaced the bombed-out roof I had seen when I first arrived there all those years ago. The hole made by the mortar bomb remained in the downstairs floor as a reminder of the siege of 1968.

One of Minh's cousins, an ex-para called Thien, came to visit us from prison. Thien was doing time for deserting his unit during the South Vietnamese Army's invasion of Laos the year before. Wounded in the left arm, he had clung with three other wounded men to the underside of a helicopter which had landed in a jungle clearing to evacuate really seriously wounded men. Two or three with him had let go and fallen to their deaths. He and a comrade survived. Mme Bong said, 'I know the judge, so Thien is allowed out sometimes from Danang prison to visit his wife, who is lodging with me.' (Another example of Mme Bong's family loyalty and kindness.) The ex-para cousin was consumed with hate for the war, for the Americans, for everything. 'Damned Americans,' he growled, 'running our country.'

Running or ruining? The Viet Cong, it struck me, were simply too *Vietnamese* for the Americans. Vietnamese peasants are accustomed to living up to their thighs in mud, they are born to the soil, to driving water buffaloes through the paddy (a particular source of scorn to Americans who spoke contemptuously of 'the goddam Vietnamese peasants who spend their youth staring up the backsides of buffaloes'), but ultimately knowing every inch of their land. It was their country. The Americans were strangers – too big, careless and loud. Even those Americans brought up as farm boys were strangers to the jungle. They were baffled by the language, made uneasy by it and infuriated by Vietnamese remoteness.

A thought I had: one thing American generals and the American 'New Left' had in common was a passionate belief in the use of force for political ends. I was thinking of the Minutemen and the Black Panthers – the civilians in the United States who protested against the Vietnam war. The utter devastation of the city of Quang Tri: that's what remains of the political game the international Left (communism) and Right (American democracy) are playing for all those self-righteous airs they proclaim so loudly. 'I never knew a man who had better motives for all the trouble he caused,' Greene said of his creation, young Alden Pyle who used bombs that blew off arms and legs, disembowelled and decapitated civilians in Saigon squares in order to promote what he thought of American ideals in Vietnam – National Democracy, a Third Force. Later, the same thing could be said not just of an innocent like Pyle but of the whole American civilian and military establishment.

Still on the subject of Pyle, Greene goes on, 'You cannot blame the innocent, they are always guiltless. All you can do is control them or eliminate them.' And his conclusion is that 'Innocence is a kind of insanity'. Well, innocence and arrogance on a grand scale *is* a kind of insanity; a madness that can kill and maim, at that.

I took advantage of the ceasefire – worked out in a far-off conference in Paris between the Americans and the communists – to meet some of the Viet Cong at last.

I had waited eight years to meet the six men who padded silently across a dusty field and shook my hand. They wore dark green uniforms and their guns were balanced on their shoulders. Their officer had a bullet-shattered arm and the grave face of a worker-priest. A few years later I was to see how hard the hearts were of these lean, saintly-looking men.

Now this man gave me a thin, priestly smile, and when I asked one of his men what his medal was for, he replied in an offhand way, 'For killing twelve Americans.' The Viet Cong officer had served in the National Liberation Front for seventeen years, he told me. He had been captured in 1958 and did eight years in prison. Later, he said, he had been three times wounded. Perhaps his wounds and his imprisonment had embittered him so much that he longed to get his own back; and probably, when the opportunity finally arrived, he did so – on people like Mme Bong's family. Yet for the moment the accent was on reconciliation. A message tied to a solitary reed, stuck upright in the dust, said simply, 'Soldiers, let us put aside vengeance. We need reconstruction now and friendship'. Now one can see in ironic retrospect that the NLF (or the Viet Cong, or the communist top brass in Hanoi) had in fact no intention of 'putting aside vengeance'. They simply wanted victory; hence the accent they sensibly put on 'friendship' now. There was little sign of it twelve years later. Today, twenty-two years later – at last – it has returned. As for 'reconstruction', that too had to wait for nearly twenty years after their victory in 1975. By that time 'vengeance' had run its course unchecked: there had been plenty of vengeance.

Peace takes getting used to, like war. It was difficult enough to like the fictional Pyles and the real-life American colonels and generals who followed him and zapped their way about Vietnam. But it was not much easier to take to those left-wing idealists who lolled comfortably (so to speak) on their spiritual roof gardens in New York, Paris and London, and hailed the approaching victory of the communists. Yes, things take getting used to; and, to do them justice, many on both sides did change their tune later.

In the American military compound in Hué, the few remaining GIs were sitting about, drinking up the cases of whisky that remained. They had nothing to do now; there was no way they could be drawn back into battle – the American invasion was on its way out. There was a tawdry end-of-term look about the nearly abandoned buildings, the ramshackle cinema with its sign, 'Perfume Picture Palace', the sandbags on the roof from which I had seen an angry American colonel directing mortar-fire into the heart of Hué in Tet 1968. It was the end of an epoch. The end of one nightmare, although no doubt other nightmares waited round the corner.

Still, these were happier times now that the shooting had stopped, if only for the time being.

I went with Mme Bong to the tomb of her son Van, near Tu Dam. There were some Christian graves in the cemetery and some without any headstones at all. 'One of those stoneless graves belongs to an army captain I knew,' said Mme Bong. 'His widow is too poor to have one made. Isn't that sad?'

Among gravestones chipped by bullets from the Tet of 1968, Mme Bong bowed, lit incense sticks and placed them before the inscription ('Tran Dinh Van. Born 15–5–1943. Died for his country 7–6–1967') on her son's tomb.

Then with her daughter and tiny granddaughter, who for the occasion wore two pink bows on her pigtails, we went off for an outing to the garden tombs of the kings of Annam – Tu Duc, Khai Dinh and Minh Mang. The ornamental ponds around those antique arches and mausoleums were full of lilies, often pink-red blooms on a single long stalk that *en masse* looked like sleeping flamingoes, and large open lotus buds. Trees and flowers surrounded the ponds – spreading cedars and heavy-smelling frangipanis, thick grasses and straggling bushes with heavy rust-coloured leaves. Creepers climbed over everything and an old guide left over from the days of real peace – how long ago was that? – led us round. He looked like an ancient mandarin himself, in his solar topee, wide cotton pants and a long, shift-like garment buttoned at the neck: a gentle figure from the past.

Here, I thought, in the peace that at last reigned so blissfully among the vivid green fields, the water, the temples, and the royal tombs of Annam, was something much nearer the essence of Vietnam than anything the ideological loudspeaker vans of Hanoi or Saigon could speak of. Something indescribably valuable was here, conveying, I believed – and still believe – to all the Mme Bongs, the Minhs and Qués: 'Peace and conciliation are all that matter. Here among this beauty is common sense. All the rest, all the ferocious babble, all the ideological talk from North or South, is a corruption.'

At such times peace seemed to envelop us like an unexpected, glorious spring. 'Perhaps at last, at last,' laughed Mme Bong, clapping her hands back in the house in Hué, 'the shooting is over for ever.'

Minh and Qué arrived on leave from Danang, and with their friends Ngoc and Tam, and of course Vua (who had leave of absence from his wife), we spent the night on a sampan on the Perfume River as we had when I first met them. The Vietnamese played guitars and Vua sang a Beatles song (I think it was 'Michelle') in my honour, some of them swam in the warm water of the river, and we bought tea and beer and food from small floating stalls, whose owners paddled them alongside. For once the flashes of gunfire running round the horizon were absent. We landed again as the sun came up, smiling at each other in something near heaven.

Chapter 5

Someone has said that, like smells or certain sounds, envelopes are remembered things.

There was never any mistaking letters from Mme Bong. I have found a letter from her written to me from Hué in June 1973, in the middle of the treacherous year of the short – the too short – ceasefire in Vietnam. In it, she talked of the approaching marriage of Qué.

Qué's wedding is fixed for 6 September 1973 at Qui Nhon. His parents want the celebrations to be very simple, that is to say, they will not invite everybody even from the family. I will miss the occasion myself, and I will be sad. But I must respect the wishes of his parents.

I do hope, though, that you will come to Minh's wedding – your honourable presence will give such pleasure. I too shall be very happy to see you again. Minh will get married at the beginning of December, but we aren't sure yet of the date. So I will send a telegram to London to warn you.

You understand what I say, don't you, dear M. Gavin?

The envelope betrayed the fact that it came from her. I recognized the firm writing with its old-fashioned loops at once, before I caught sight of the stamp and the Hué postmark.

She had added a postscript:

*Finally, why did you forget to send the photos of our visit to the royal
tombs in Hué? Have you lost the film? If that has happened I should
be very sad. I thought you would pay attention to these things. But,*
enfin, *you are so far away, so far from us that I cannot be angry with
you. So please don't worry about anything,* cher Monsieur.

So Mme Bong was angry with me because of the missing photographs.
That showed that at last I had achieved some sort of genuine compat-
ibility with the rest of her family. Funnily enough that thought made
me extraordinarily happy.

I hope by now I have described the Bong family sufficiently well to
have conveyed the fact that they were poor victims of circumstance –
like so many Vietnamese of that time. They certainly were not rich;
nor, it must be said, were they destitute. They, like many other ordinary
Vietnamese, wanted only to get on with their peaceful humdrum lives,
and of course that was the one thing they were not allowed to do.

The war prevented that. The war, that had started way back in 1945
before many of them were born, swept them up willy-nilly in a fatal
maelstrom. The young men of the family were obliged to put on the
uniform that in the end branded them as candidates for years in
communist prison camps – a uniform they hated to wear, although as
conscripts they were obliged to. I imagine Ho Trang, Mme Bong's
son-in-law, was the only really dedicated servant of Saigon in the family,
and the boldest and bravest. He was the only one of the family to rise
to be anything as exalted as a lieutenant-colonel in the South Vietnamese
Army, far outstripping the others – Minh, for example, whose sister
he married. He was the one who became a district chief near Nha
Trang. He was a determined anti-communist and, during the ceasefire
truce of 1973, when someone asked him if he would sit down and drink
tea with the Viet Cong, he was horrified by the very idea, and snapped,
'Drink tea with the Viet Cong? My orders from Saigon say not to

fraternize. If the Viet Cong come here, I shall shoot them.' He would always obey orders; he was like that.

Mme Bong, I hope I have shown, was quite different; with her, family always comes first. Even so, Ho Trang did not deserve to be lost for seven years in a re-education camp. Nobody deserved that. Certainly not Minh or Qué who suffered the same fate as Ho Trang. But it was Ho Trang, as we shall see, who chiefly helped his family – and Minh's – to find a new life in exile in the United States when the communists made it impossible for them to remain in their own country. Of course, he would have preferred to live out his life in Vietnam. But, in the end, their exile was his essential contribution to the family's well-being.

People may ask why I am writing about this family at all. The answer – I hope it's an obvious one – is that I came to love and to feel a great compassion for them. I want others to think of them, too; and to know what it was like then – in that time of what seemed like endless war.

It so happened that after this short period of peace and heaven on earth in Vietnam came the bitterest time of all. A time that lasted the best part of twenty years.

I left Vietnam sometime in early 1974. My newspaper sent me to Africa, to cover Angola and Mozambique, where African nationalists were fighting the Portuguese. The world outside Vietnam did not stand still, more's the pity, and after my African period I had to return to Portugal when that country itself erupted on the death of Dr Salazar, its long-lived dictator. Things there took some time to settle down. I was in Cyprus on leave, recovering from these exhausting and violent events, when the Turkish army suddenly stormed across the sea from the mainland into the northern parts of this largely Greek island, eventually dividing it up for a few decades (until this day, in fact).

So it was in Cyprus, on the other side of the world, that I was compelled to read about the collapse of the South Vietnamese Army;

its pell-mell rout; the fall of Hué and Danang; the communists' lightning advance through the Central Highlands and down the coastal plain south of Danang, the flight of Generals Thieu and Ky, and the eventual surrender of Saigon. The TV stations of the West, including Cyprus, showed these events day by day, and they culminated in shots of the American embassy in Saigon as hysterical hordes of weeping Vietnamese civilians tried to escape on the last American helicopters, even trying to crash their cars through the barriers at the airport. It made for horrific, bitter, devastating viewing. I was beside myself. I didn't know what to do. The unexpected Turkish invasion of Cyprus, full of fire and bloodshed as it was, was child's play to me compared with what I imagined was going on in Vietnam – and to the Bong family. But I had to stick to the Turkish invasion and report on it. Where *was* Mme Bong now, I wondered? Where were Minh and Qué?

At last one day an envelope arrived with the remembered writing on it – Mme Bong's writing. It was a deeply sad letter, and, in its dignity, a frightening one. I had never received such a letter of despair from her before; despair was the last thing I associated with Mme Bong. The letter (in French, of course) was written in Saigon and began:

My very dear M. Gavin [it was the first time she had addressed me so warmly],

It is a very sad thing to have to tell you our news. Everything is lost now. My very dear, my only son, Minh, was in Danang. He is with the communists, but at a time like this, I cannot imagine – can he still be alive? Or is he dead already? It is so, so sad, unimaginable for a poor mother.

I cannot express my feelings because we live from minute to minute. Our grandchildren and their parents are all in Saigon. I have no more tears left to weep for my little Minh and at the same time for my grandchildren. Ah, my country, my poor country.

*I send you my most tender and affectionate friendship. And adieu –
my very dear Monsieur Gavin.*

Perhaps this is the last letter I shall send you.

Adieu.

It must be the saddest letter I have ever received. I sat in the hotel
in faraway Nicosia, and read it again and again. There was nothing I
could do about it. What was the point even in answering it? My letter
would never reach her. Nor could I go back. The communists were in
control now. They had won a total victory, and my friends were their
prisoners.

Almost at once, though, another letter arrived from Saigon. It came
from my friend and successor in Vietnam, the correspondent from my
newspaper who visited Vietnam when I was away for the moment at
some other war. Mark Frankland was one of the best journalists of
that time on any newspaper. He too had fallen half in love with the
country and its people; he had met Mme Bong and got on well with
her, and with Qué, Minh and Vua. It had been his ill-luck to have to
stay behind while the collapse of the South Vietnamese Army took
place, to have to witness the panicked confusion of the entry of the
communists into Saigon and the increasing panic and confusion that
took place after that.

Now came his letter, which I fell upon like a starving puppy grabbing
a juicy bone.

*I was walking down Tu Do [Street] when I heard a voice shouting my
name – Vua – who else? A minute later Mme Bong went by on the
back of a scooter driven by the District Chief son-in-law from Nha
Trang [Ho Trang] (whom you met in 1973). I went to their house (off
the Bien Hoa highway and surrounded by houses and disused paddy
fields) for dinner.*

Mme B is in a terrible state about Minh being in Danang; says she cannot live with the communists; talks of taking cyanide. Qué's wife is also in Danang. Minh had risen to being Assistant Province Chief for Quang Tri – unfortunately.

Vua's father and some other relations managed to get a helicopter out of Danang, but it was either shot down or ran out of fuel in Binh Dinh – they may be still alive. Vua is adapting to the new situation, busy keeping what's left of his family together. His mother is in Saigon, ill with cancer. His wife and two daughters are in Can Tho [in the Delta] while he works for a branch of the Agricultural Ministry. He still jokes. And is rather admirable – very good with poor Mme Bong.

The house is full of little children. Minh's wife and the elder son's [Van's] wife are there. So is the Nha Trang District Chief [Ho Trang] and his family. They have little hope of getting out, for they have no claim on the Americans. I don't believe a mass evacuation of 200,000 is possible. Vua, at any rate, is resigned to staying.

They have enough money. All one can do is go and see them, listen to their troubles. It is a horrible mess. Saigon is full of people like them . . .

I was worried because I had heard – I can't think now where I had heard it or how – that Minh had been wounded by a shell splinter. A shell splinter, I thought, could be more painful than a bullet; its velocity can shock and numb. But there were more serious considerations. I thought of the months in hospital such a wound might entail. I knew those field hospitals only too well. I had spent the best part of two days on two separate occasions in a military hospital in Can Tho and had seen unbelievable squalor. Some of the busiest wards were simply long Nissen huts with low curved ceilings of corrugated iron without air conditioning. These seemed to collect and reflect the heat, so the heat inside them was truly appalling despite a few slowly turning fans.

Wire mesh across the windows was designed to keep mosquitoes at bay, but where it was torn or where the corners had rusted away, the mosquitoes poured in. There were two or three wounded men to most of the small beds here, lying side by side in their filth with, above their bloody, bandaged bodies, the drip-feed machines and all the suspended paraphernalia of a hospital for the seriously injured. The smell in that heat, as one can imagine, leave alone the sights, made one's stomach churn. Yet relatives of the wounded cluttered the narrow spaces between the beds and in some cases seemed to be permanently camped there, babies and all.

That was Can Tho hospital in wartime. So what would Danang be like in the hurly-burly of confusion and fear of the communist takeover and the panic flight of everybody else? Would there be any nurses left? Any doctors? Eventually, to my intense relief, the story of Minh's wound proved false – but for a nasty day or two, wrestling with the horrors of mass graves in Cyprus, I got little or no sleep, lying awake thinking of the consequences of that shell splinter for Minh and for his poor suicidal mother.

One other consideration worried me. It was, it seemed to me, an overriding factor in this appalling situation – I wrote about it in my newspaper shortly before the communist victory; it was connected with 'face', the 'face' of the South Vietnamese as much as that of the communists in Hanoi. The scars of war went, it seemed to me, very deep; exemplified, for example, by Ho Trang (the District Chief's) refusal to fraternize with the Viet Cong during the ceasefire. In the years following the communists' victory, the extreme depth of those scars, of that irreconcilability would become very apparent.

The peaceful, beautiful Vietnam I had caught glimpses of in Hué, particularly with Mme Bong on those expeditions that took us among the ancient fish ponds, royal tombs and flower gardens across the river – I thought I knew that that Vietnam persisted in all Vietnamese hearts, but I had no idea if it could survive everything that was going on now. I rather thought not. That that face of Vietnam was there all right, I knew; I could feel it hovering almost palpably about us; it always hung about in the background. It was as intangible as smoke. It had nothing whatsoever to do with the Americans – interlopers who had been in the country a mere decade. It had no political power. So, like a rare and beautiful butterfly, it was vulnerable; it could be crushed between the armed forces of selfish international idealists of right or left, whose very idealism could lead to a machine-gun burst in someone else's stomach, and oblige a harmless widow like Mme Bong to comb a remote battlefield for chunks of her son to scoop into a plastic bag and carry home.

With the fall of Saigon I was left to contemplate the memory of my friends in Vietnam, not knowing if they were still alive or about to be shot.

Would the communists shoot Qué in the army uniform he hated so much? Would Mme Bong take cyanide as she had apparently threatened to do? I don't claim that my friends represented all Vietnamese from the North to the South. Far from it. There were even differences of opinion within the Bong family (the uncompromising views of Ho Trang versus those of Qué, for example). But all of them were my friends. I had seen how they, like millions of others, had been trapped between two forces they had absolutely no time for: the cruelty and corruption of communism and the corruption, incompetence and repression of America's protégés – the Vietnamese officers in Saigon. Well, now the quicksands of defeat were lapping the innocent heads of that family from Hué.

It didn't seem as much as ten years ago that I had met Vua on that Air Vietnam plane to Hué. Or did it? So much had happened since then, including much that I have not had space to recount here: all the trivia of day-to-day friendship.

I had been right to come to Hué early on. Hué had something more than beauty; it had an antique pride – faded, admittedly, but still beguiling. Of course, it had seen better days. Hué people knew this better than anyone and clung for consolation to their pure form of nationalism. Neutralism – which the Americans foolishly equated with communism – was stronger here than anywhere in South Vietnam – it was not surprising that Hué was out of bounds to American troops. No one much missed Bao Dai, the departed emperor (certainly not Mme Bong and 'my' family), but Hué's population, easily inflamed and led by Buddhist monks in saffron robes, had boiled out into the streets to help bring down the stiff-necked, Buddhist-hating Catholic dictator in Saigon, Ngo Dinh Diem. Later, when his intellectual younger brother, Nhu, and Diem himself were dead, assassinated, and when his regime had, by force, been superseded by General Thieu and Air Vice-Marshal Nguyen Cao Ky – both backed by the Americans – the independent-minded Hué people turned on them, too; partly because they represented a foreign power – America; partly for their perceived incompetence and corruption.

As we now know, Hué's 'resistance' was futile in the end, despite Hué's refusal to support the communists when they occupied the city in the Tet holidays of 1968. Minh and Qué – and all the others who had taken part in the Buddhist uprising and had even gone to the barricades to protest the political shenanigans in Saigon, as Thich Tri Quang had urged them to – were obliged to go into the South Vietnamese Army like everybody else. And when the communists won the war, they suffered for that: they were accused of unspecified 'war guilt' and 'war crimes' – although they had killed no one – and were sentenced accordingly to long terms in re-education camps. That is to say, their lives were ruined.

It was to be a very long time before I saw any of them again. Let me be exact: ten years went by after I had received Mme Bong's letter of despair. Ten whole years during which I had no news of her family whatever. For all I knew, they might have vanished from the earth.

I had to wait until 1985, the tenth anniversary of the fall of Saigon. And then one day I received an official Vietnamese government invitation to

attend the great parade they intended to hold in Saigon to celebrate
their victory. Just as important as the parade to me was the fact that
the invitation included a visit to Hanoi – that is where the week's tour
started – and also a guided trek down the coast to Hué and Danang,
then to Saigon for the parade, and finally to My Tho on the way to
the Delta. I was free to accept, and luckily for me the management of
my newspaper agreed that I should go.

The tour, I noted, was to be a guided one, which meant the constant
presence of a communist minder who would lurk at my shoulder to
make sure I spoke only to the 'right' people and saw the 'right' things.
Still, I wanted at all costs to go back to this country I had been separated
from for far too long – and incidentally (no, *in particular*) to try to
find out what had happened to Mme Bong and her family. For a start,
were they alive? I didn't know even that.

Although I was given the honour of watching the parade, I knew I
was also being invited back to see how efficiently the superhuman
victors of the war (they thought of themselves precisely as that) were
guiding their country in times of the peace they had imposed and now,
by all accounts, maintained by dire repression. At that time the sole
friend in the whole world of the new rulers of Vietnam was the
poverty-stricken Soviet Union, which had lost little time in appropriat-
ing a former American base at Cam Ranh Bay – a deep port on the
South China Sea – to the alarm of China, which loathed the Soviet
Union almost as much as it did the Russians' new ally, the People's
Republic of Vietnam.

I should have known what to expect. I was going to a communist-
dominated country. I should have been prepared for what I found.

Nevertheless I had no idea of the state I would find the country in.
Nor had I any idea of the police-state horrors that I would be subjected
to, or persecution which would soon drive most of the Bong family out
of their own country and into exile.

Part Two

CELEBRATION 1985

Yet there is no great problem in the world today
Except disease and death men cannot end
If no man tries to dominate another.
The struggle for material existence is over. It has been won.
The need for repressions and disciplines has passed.

Hugh MacDiarmid: 'Lament for Great Music'

Chapter 6

How did I know without any doubt – just by looking at my opened door – that someone had ransacked my hotel room while I was out having dinner in Hanoi? I had only been in the place a few hours on the first night of my tour – an official tour – of Vietnam. I had arrived as an official guest in Hanoi from Bangkok that evening in April 1985.

I had already been warned by fellow-journalists who had been there fairly recently that Vietnamese at that time suffered an almost total lack of many basic necessities: things like soap, shaving cream, toothbrushes, toothpaste, were completely lacking. So I had filled a pillowcase full of such things before leaving Bangkok (I had been told I could bring them in to Vietnam), and had declared them all at Hanoi airport to a number of surprisingly hostile customs officers in colonial-type pith helmets. Outside the airport my minder was waiting for me. I would like to forget all about him, but there is no possibility of my doing that.

Mr Thai was a bony man of indeterminate age and unprepossessing aspect, a misanthropic character whose teeth had seen better days and whose breath, I very soon discovered sitting close to him in the back of the official car, was simply unbearable. So much did Mr Thai's breath worry me that I fumbled in my pillowcase there and then to produce two toothbrushes and two tubes of Colgate. These I handed to Mr Thai, saying, 'Please, Mr Thai. I hear that Vietnam is short of these things. Please accept one for yourself and one for your wife, if you have one.'

Mr Thai's reaction was twofold. First, he seemed to think I had offered him a bribe: second, he began to protest that Vietnam lacked absolutely nothing that was freely available in the outside world. His protestations did honour to his ideology, but were so forceful and at the same time so mendacious that I almost grabbed back the toothbrushes and paste. His protests did not, by the way, include a rejection of 'the bribe'. Nevertheless we had only met a few moments ago and we were at the start of a whole week's tour together. So I let it go.

At least I knew where I stood with Mr Thai from that moment. If he was 'us', I was 'them'. It remained that way until I left Saigon airport seven or eight days later. It was not, one might say, the ideal combination of guide and guided.

When I complimented him on his English, Mr Thai said he had learned it in Reading, England, where he had for some reason been studying the language – no doubt, I thought perhaps unfairly, the better to be able to persecute British visitors to his country. At any rate, he now became known to me – and I put it into the account of all this I sent to my newspaper – as Mr Thai Reading. Now I try to forget Mr Thai; if I had taken him as typical, I would have been put off Vietnamese for ever.

The first evening I had time for just a quick look at Hanoi, a brief ramble round shops that looked as empty of everything as I had been led to believe – of smiles, too. I found it hard to believe that the communists had managed to eliminate Vietnamese smiles from their country; those smiles had been so ubiquitous. I returned disconsolately to my grand hotel; I was invited out to dinner by some diplomats.

Later that night, a worse thing was to befall me in that hotel.

That evening I had been invited to meet one of the Western ambassadors – not the American or the British (as a matter of fact, I don't think there was a British ambassador in Hanoi just then; perhaps he was simply away on leave). Instead I had a most unsatisfactory conversation in the office of some other English-speaking representative – unsatisfactory because he said he thought everything in Vietnam was going wonderfully well. The communists had been 'brilliant' in war, he said (brilliant was obviously a word he cherished), now they were going to be 'brilliant' in peace. We could learn from them, he said.

Soon he was saying things like, 'Let me tell you a true story. Just the other day, I was upcountry visiting an old pagoda, a rather beautiful one, I must say. There were some Vietnamese pilgrims there. They were smiling and having a great time. You could see from their smiles that they thought things were going pretty well. See what I mean?'

No. I didn't quite see what he meant, and I said so.

'A few smiles from pilgrims on a visit to a pagoda? And you reported that back to your Foreign Ministry? With the rather sweeping conclusions you have drawn about the success of the communist peace?'

He didn't like the disbelief in my voice. 'How long have you been in Vietnam?' he asked sharply. And when I said I had that very afternoon arrived from Bangkok, he smiled a little smile behind his desk.

'You'll be going south, I imagine,' he said at last.

'Yes. Two days here in Hanoi. A day in Hué, another in Danang. Then Saigon – sorry, Ho Chi Minh City.' It was going to take a while for me to get used to calling Saigon by its new name. 'Then the victory celebrations. I am not sure how long I will be there. It depends what day the parade is. Perhaps four or five days. Perhaps longer.'

A Vietnamese army parade was scheduled through the streets of Saigon to celebrate the North's victory ten years before. Mr Thai would tell me the date and the time. The words 'liberation' and 'reunification' were already being bandied about in Hanoi; there were street signs emphasizing them, and Mr Thai had used both words several times in the car from the airport.

'Perhaps we'll meet there, then,' the ambassador said without warmth. Why should anyone blame him, confronted as he was by an English journalist he had never set eyes on, and one, what's more, who had only just arrived from – God knows where?

I went on to my dinner date, and eventually returned to my hotel.

It was now that it happened. I can only repeat my earlier question and answer it myself.

How did I know that someone had – very crudely – searched my room while I was out? For a start there was part of a heel mark in smudged talcum powder on the carpet outside the door. The door itself didn't look quite shut, and sure enough when I gave it a gentle push with my fingertips, it swung open of its own accord. I didn't need to reach for the key in my trouser pocket.

Inside, the room was a shambles: a shambles of spilled toothpaste, smeared Lux and Lifebuoy soap, toothbrushes covered with sticky Bovril, scattered all over the place, mixed with piles of smeared razor blades. Shaving cream canisters, slashed with knives, had leaked into a can of Danish liver pâté; shaving cream was everywhere, over the bedsheets, the blankets, and even occasionally the walls. Tubes – of toothpaste, for example – had been punctured with needles, and soapcakes slashed apart with razor blades or knives. My pillowcase had been emptied, the contents searched and pillaged. The remains were scattered about the room, even on its walls and floor.

The room was a hopeless mess. It had been made virtually uninhabit-able. But a single moment's thought told me it wasn't worth my while to see the receptionist and make a fuss. The receptionist, I guessed, would be perfectly aware of what had happened; he had probably handed over my room key to the police.

I cleared a space on the wrecked bed to sit down, and pondered the situation.

Obviously the search had been done so crudely for one of two reasons: either the Vietnamese secret police were extremely ham-fisted; or they had wanted to make an obvious point – to warn me. Warn me of what? Not to try to overthrow the regime? If all it took to overthrow the Vietnamese communist regime, which had defeated the American giant plus America's allies in the South, was a single British journalist, there must be something dangerously wrong with that regime.

Of course, the police might not see it that way. So if it was a warning, plain and simple, I was prepared to let it go at that. What else could I do?

I could not, at any rate, take umbrage, drive out to the airport in high dudgeon and demand to be flown back to Bangkok. I had a job to do: I had been sent here by my newspaper to report the story, and space had been reserved for my long piece to appear in the paper in two or three weeks' time. I could not, however much I wanted to, flounce out of Hanoi in a fuming rage.

All I could do was to meet Mr Thai Reading next morning as he had arranged; I would get on with his programme, without so much as mentioning the room search. I only hoped that the hotel maid would somehow clean up my room in my absence at Ho Chi Minh's mausoleum, which, as Mr Thai said with Uriah Heep-style unction, was our most important port of call that day.

Important it obviously was to him as well as the long line of Vietnamese visitors and foreign tourists herded by barking guards to queue for a sight of the mummified body of Ho Chi Minh under glass, floodlit below the hammer and sickle on the wall.

It was only ten years later that I realized that this whole hideous mausoleum was a Leninist lie, imposed by Russia on the Vietnamese communist rulers (and accepted by them) against the wishes expressed before he died by 'Uncle Ho' himself. He had said in writing that he wished to be burned, Buddhist-style, and to have his ashes scattered around the Vietnamese countryside that he loved. Ho was a simple

83

man in many ways, and this heavy Soviet-style monstrosity of a mauso-leum was not to his taste at all.

Sure enough, by the time we had gazed at the corpse of Ho Chi Minh under its spotlight and returned to the hotel, my room had been cleaned up. I heard nothing ever again about the previous night's chaotic search. The next morning Mr Thai and I drove back to Hanoi airport for our flight south to Danang in a ramshackle Soviet jet which had no overhead lockers or seatbelts, so that we sat hugging our bags on our knees while mannish stewardesses forced big cardboard boxes under our legs. It was an agonizing and frightening flight.

I can't remember much about our visit to Danang. Mr Thai's driver tried, having somehow given his temporary boss the slip, to get me to change some black market dollars for him which, in that miserable time, I could only take to be one encouraging sign of the survival of the spirit of independence of individual Vietnamese.

I can't remember if I obliged him. I doubt it. The thought of seeing Hué again dominated my thoughts to the exclusion of all else. Would I find Mme Bong there? I wondered. I really had no idea where she was; I feared she might have sold everything and moved to Saigon. How I would find her there in that sprawling city I had no idea.

Mr Thai had instructions to get me a room in the very hotel in which I had crouched with my whisky bottle in 1972, the time of the North Vietnamese Army's offensive down the coastal plain, the Street Without Joy, the time the market had been burned by South Vietnamese deserters, the time I had been jostled outside Mme Bong's doorway. I had been almost paralysed with fear then – as I have explained, it was one of the worst nights I have ever spent. Now it was just a dreary, run-down dump of an hotel, not frightening at all, merely depressing. The recep-tionist whom I had thought might be a Viet Cong in 1972 had gone – promoted to a top post in Hanoi perhaps? – and the timid girl in his place shared the dim, sad dreariness of the hotel itself.

From my room I looked out over the Perfume River at the newly built market that blocked my view of the street where Mme Bong's house stood. How, I wondered, was I going to make a reasonable excuse to get there? I couldn't leave Mr Thai behind; it was more than his life was worth to let me out of his sight for five minutes. Nevertheless that I was back in Hué filled me with hope and a new-found elation. There on that river, we had spent all those wartime nights – I and those Vietnamese who later had become part of my life. Were they still here? That was the important question. I had heard nothing of them since the disintegration and chaos of 1975. I had received no letter, no smuggled message. Either they had been among missing boat people, refugees who had drowned in the South China Sea, or they were somewhere in Vietnam. Perhaps they were here, in Hué.

During the time it had taken for my visa to come through (it took a year) I had more than once repeated my reasons for wanting to go south from Hanoi: I wanted to see old friends, I said, being particularly careful not to mention their names or former addresses in case the secret police stage-managed a meeting. To see old friends – the press department people nodded vaguely, finding my request tiresomely eccentric. 'To see old friends – what on earth for?'

Nevertheless here I was at last bounding across the familiar bridge over the Perfume River with a reluctant Mr Thai alongside me, heading for the little doorway through which I had found sanctuary so many times in the nine years I had spent in Vietnam during the American war. In the end I had induced Mr Thai to cross the bridge, and once opposite the house I just dived in through that doorway. I was in luck – of a sort. There, facing me, was Mme Bong. She stood staring at me as though I was a ghost, in an almost empty room. And, in amazement and shock, I stared back.

I was as shocked by that sudden sight of her as she seemed shocked to see me. She seemed to have shrunk as, unsmiling, she led me to a small, bare table; and for some time we sat there in silence on the hard chairs as if it were visiting time in a jail. I noticed she kept glancing fearfully about her, and after a time she whispered, 'This is too danger-ous.' I saw she was particularly worried about Mr Thai. She kept looking at him furtively. 'The communists . . . the terror,' she could only mutter in my ear, and I felt I had stepped into an Orwellian adventure in an alien police state. I began to think that even Mr Thai felt pity for Mme Bong when he said, 'Have a talk', and moved away. But he didn't go far: only to a chair in a corner.

There wasn't much time. I asked at once, 'Where's Minh?'

'In Saigon.' Her whisper was barely audible. 'He was seven years in a re-education camp. Qué too.' Close to, I could see new lines in her face; she looked as though she had come to the end of her tether. She looked weary and haunted.

And what she had said horrified me.

I thought of Qué with his long face and lopsided grin; the face that reminded me of Smike. I remembered his long silences and his sad thoughtfulness, his love of *The Grapes of Wrath* and Albert Camus; and I thought of him, sick and sad, enduring seven years – more than 2,500 days – in a remote re-education camp. I wasn't so worried about Minh. He was a different matter. He was an extrovert – forthright, humorous, talkative. He might have fared better in those isolated circumstances. Still it would have been very hard for both of them. Seven years!

'How is Minh?' I asked.

'Minh is destitute.'

'What does he do?'

She paused. 'He is a . . . coolie . . .' From her hesitation, I could see there was more to it than that.

'Shall I see him in Saigon?'

'No, no. It is too dangerous.'

When I said that he had served his prison sentence – he had paid for his so-called crimes, he must be free to see me now – she only repeated, 'Too dangerous. Too dangerous.'

A pause and she added, 'Minh has a son aged eleven, and a second son aged two.'

Mr Thai suddenly chipped in (perhaps he had been listening after all). 'Has this lady a husband?' he asked.

'She had,' I said. 'He was with the Viet Minh. He died.' I wasn't going to stop there. 'She was with the Viet Minh, too.'

He looked at me with a disbelieving sneer. 'Oh,' he said.

'Oh yes. She was in the forests with the Viet Minh. It's not only the communists who fought for a free Vietnam, you know, Mr Thai. You haven't got a monopoly of patriotism.'

Mr Thai kept quiet after that.

I had a thought: perhaps re-education had worked only too well. I said, 'Perhaps Minh doesn't *want* to see me.'

'How can you say that,' Mme Bong demanded in a furious and trembling voice. And then she began to cry. I had never considered the possibility that Mme Bong would cry about anything. When she burst into tears the effect was unbelievably shocking.

'The emotion,' she said when she had recovered herself.

In this state of shock, we sat there for a short time longer without talking, until Mr Thai from his corner said it was time to go. Mme Bong and I looked at each other. Our past lay about us in the cold, silent room in which it seemed to me that half my life had been spent. I noticed the break in the cement floor where the mortar bomb had fallen during Tet 1968. Even that was seventeen years ago.

In a day or two, to attend the parade to mark the tenth anniversary of the communist victory, Mr Thai and I went on down to Saigon. For the Grand Parade, Mr Thai told me we should leave the hotel at 6.00 a.m. because the President of Vietnam had to welcome 1100 guests and the speech the Mayor of Ho Chi Minh City had planned should start at 7.00 a.m. and last about twenty minutes. Then there would be a reading of a government decision to award Ho Chi Minh City the Order of the Gold Star (something no one mentions now, as far as I know). After that there would be a playing of the national anthem and a twenty-one gun salute. Then the parade itself would begin. I was even given the order of the parade by Mr Thai:

1. Infantry
2. Motorcyclists
3. Artillery
4. Missiles
5. Tanks
6. Aeroplanes
7. Civilian parade 'of the masses'

I suppose only about 20,000 of the 4.3 million people in Saigon turned out to watch the parade. A few cheered the goose-stepping soldiers, or the ageing Soviet tanks or the beautiful marching girls. On a dais on one side of the street, elderly, bemedalled communist officials relentlessly smiled; on the other, across a spiritual chasm, the Saigonese 'masses' silently stared. It struck me that the communists were having a party all to themselves. I suppose the most important foreign guest there was the Cuban Foreign Minister, who spent a long time fiddling with an immense cigar as big as a six-inch gun.

A prediction I made then has come true, it seems. Reporting this sad event, I wrote: 'Do we have to wait for a younger generation in Hanoi to replace the old men, heroes in war; cruel, ideological stick-in-the-muds in peace; who have won a great victory and yet seem to hate all the world – even their own people?'

Well, we had to wait about another four years for the change. And one has to admit it was well worth waiting for.

*

By a stroke of extraordinarily good fortune, I happened to bump into my old friend Minh in Pasteur Street in Saigon. Like his mother, this once ebullient young man stood staring at me as if he had seen a particularly terrifying ghost. Like his mother he had changed; he had become another tired, grey thirty-something-year-old man in a T-shirt.

'Mr Gavin?' he said; his face was pale and rigid.

'Minh! How are you?'

As his mother had done, he kept glancing fearfully around him, scrutinizing each passer-by as though he might be a police informer. 'It is forbidden in the People's Republic of Vietnam to talk to foreigners,' he said in a toneless voice. He sounded like a record.

'I know,' I said. 'But look . . .' Quickly I gave him the name of my hotel, and my room number. I assured him that I had seen his mother in Hué and that an official would be in touch with him soon.

'Perhaps we can meet for dinner in a day or two,' I said. Minh's face was a parody of fear; I had never encountered anything quite like this. I knew I was the cause of that fear. Our dinner did take place but not before there had been a mysterious mix-up over that, too. According to Mr Thai, Minh would appear at my hotel – the Palace I think it was – at five o'clock. Two days later Minh did not come at five or even six, and after a while Mr Thai got fed up and left me. Minh came, alone, at eight. I will never know if he had really been told to show up at eight as he said, or if simple fear had driven the hour of five completely out of his head. At any rate, I left messages for Mr Thai (I didn't want any accusations of underhand dealings on my part to come from him) and took Minh up to the hotel restaurant where he ordered a beer and a steak. He looked uneasy there, too, although now he managed to smile once or twice. He mentioned that he thought the cashier and a waiter were paying us unusual attention, and presently, leaving most of his steak untouched, Minh said, 'I'm going now. It's better.'

He went, but I had learned a lot at that restaurant table. First, Qué

was outside Saigon at Bien Hoa. He was terribly poor, said Minh –
could I do something for him? He was working non-stop as a labourer
in some agricultural project and ruining his health.

At the time of the South Vietnamese collapse in 1975, Minh said, he
and Qué had both been in Danang and had escaped, but had been
picked up by the communist police at the house in Hué three days later.
The re-education camp had followed – seven years of imprisonment.
There had been a period of rigorous hard labour, he said, interspersed
with lectures on Marxism-Leninism, and 'correct thinking'.

Neither he nor Qué had been tortured, Minh assured me – no physical
abuse, only back-breaking hard labour month after month, year after
year. The food was barely adequate, he said, but his wife had been
able to visit him every two months for fifteen minutes, and to bring
him small food parcels.

Perhaps the most important thing he had to say was that he wanted
at all costs to get his family and himself out of Vietnam. There was,
he said, a programme by which it was possible to leave legally. But
Vietnamese needed sponsorship. 'I'll look into that at once,' I told him.
'Don't worry.' But it took years for poor Minh to emigrate to the
United States.

Various friends – people I knew from Hué – had escaped already.
'You remember Ngoc? He escaped to Australia. Oh,' Minh said, 'and
Vua tried three times to take a boat out, was caught each time, and
jailed, too.'

'So what are you doing for a living now, Minh?' I asked for perhaps
the fourth time. 'Where are you working?' I find it difficult to describe
his extreme diffidence. 'Look, we have been friends for twenty years.
You used to say I was your elder brother.' It was shame, of course,
that had gripped him. 'You may work in the sewers – so what? I shall
understand,' I insisted. 'There is no shame now.'

But there was a lot of shame. The pain of the admission was obvious
to see. He muttered across the table in a low voice, 'I buy sweets in

the market. Small packets of sweets. Then I resell them in another part of Saigon.' He looked utterly woebegone when he added, 'The profit is so tiny, you know.' To try to lighten the atmosphere, I said, 'Well, sweets are better than sewers.' And at last he managed a laugh.

Mr Thai did not, to my surprise, lose his temper or his cool when I told him about Minh's late appearance that evening. Perhaps he knew about it already. He even agreed to allow Minh, his wife and two small sons and his sister to come to dinner with me in a newly opened and almost empty nightclub, I remember. Rats scurried over our feet and a violinist played 'Red Sails in the Sunset' over and over again. We had a joyless and indifferent meal under the tawdry decorations.

Mr Thai supervised the whole affair and with his consent I discussed what could be done for Minh and his family. They obviously had no future in their own country. Not after the stigma of re-education. The family was marked for life; they had a police dossier. There would never be any decent jobs, no places in a university for his sons – or Qué's. When Mr Thai left the room to wash his hands, Minh begged me, 'Please help them to go abroad.'

'I'll do all I can, Minh,' I promised. And leaning across the table I pressed $400 into his hand; all I had. Mr Thai returned a moment later.

I knew by now that I could only try to get them into something called the Orderly Departure Programme, designed by the Vietnamese and American governments, and approved by the UN. It was a dignified way to jettison one's country, although not an easy one. Vietnamese had begun leaving their homeland legally in mid-1979 under the ODP, as opposed to the disorderly departures of the wretched boat people, although the ODP did not stop the boat people. The new programme would enable the Politburo in Hanoi to get rid of undesirable compatriots without incurring the odium attached to the shocking flight of the boat people – a flight that still continued more than ten years after 'liberation' in 1975.

Eighty-one thousand Vietnamese had already left under the ODP. About 80,000 more were waiting for host countries to agree to receive them. A larger, unknown number had applied for exit visas from the Vietnamese Government – nothing could be done without those exit visas. I was told they could cost several thousand dollars in bribes to Vietnamese officials. Only a few thousand people were able to leave each month, so the wait to escape legally could last five years. It was a matter of painstaking screening by the Vietnamese authorities and by the host governments. Officially, priority was given to those seeking reunion with relatives already abroad, to inmates of re-education centres (though they could not qualify then because of the political impasse between Vietnam and the United States), and people already released from re-education camps. Minh and Qué, of course, might qualify for the last category.

But who would take them? America had taken the most refugees – some 200,000 in 1984 – Canada, Australia and France came next. Britain's attitude to fugitives was comparatively frosty. But perhaps wheels might be set turning on behalf of my friends. Now I had, I thought, to see Minh once more, at least so that he might give me details of his family's ages, marriages and so on. But a note appeared in my hotel mailbox the next day simply saying, 'Too busy to see you. Minh.' Obviously nonsense, this drove me wild with worry. How could Minh be too busy?

His future might be in my hands – such as it was – but what was the Government up to? Mr Thai was expressionless. When I asked him to go to see Minh, he said sharply, 'No.' When I threatened to go to Minh's house on my own, Mr Thai said, 'I advise you not to, not for your sake, but for Minh's.'

I never saw Minh again. I was not allowed to see Qué at all. I imagined a thin, worn, gentle face, and now that he was in ill health, weary, and deep in a loneliness that must seem without hope, I wanted to say to him, 'Look, there is hope, after all this time I am going to try to help. Perhaps at last – who knows – you will see the *globe terrestre* that Camus told you was so beautiful, and you will know that he was right.'

But I got the papers I needed in the end. Not everyone was heartless in communist Vietnam 1985. Mr Long from the Ho Chi Minh City press office listened to my last-minute plea for someone – anyone – to retrieve those documents without which I could do little or nothing to get any Vietnamese out of anywhere. I told him I was leaving for Bangkok the next morning. It was now or never. I wanted to leave presents and some money. Mr Long nodded. He took the presents. And he returned with a manila envelope that contained all I needed to apply for the ODP programme.

So far so good. But the outlook was depressing to say the least.

Mr Thai had lent me a booklet in Hué. It was called *Whose Human Rights?* and it was the Hanoi Government's reply to the flood of international protest on the subject of the re-education camps. A passage in it read:

Re-education and not punishment – such is the fundamental differ-ence between our system and that of other countries which con-demns the prisoner in court. By sparing him this conviction, our system spares him a stained police record which would follow him throughout his life and would even influence his children ... A re-educated person could return to a normal life.

Well, Minh and Qué were re-educated in theory, but can selling sweets and doing grinding agricultural labour be a 'normal life' for people like them? Are deliberately imposed fear and penury 'normal'? These questions haunted the last days of my visit to Vietnam in 1985. And I ended the article I sent to my newspaper as follows:

'With malice towards none, with charity for all' – Abraham Lincoln's words would have no place in the new communist Vietnam. I saw no efforts to bind up the nation's wounds; to reconcile the country. When I asked a senior official of the People's Committee in Saigon why in the much talked-of battle to rescue Vietnam's abysmal economy every human resource was not drawn upon – communist or non-communist, re-educated or not re-educated – he simply evaded the question.

The official of the People's Committee (talking to me in the Majestic) had not 'simply evaded the question'. 'Many people in the West,' he had said truthfully, 'had predicted a bloodbath after the war.' There had been none. Nearly one million of Saigon's army of administrators, he admitted, had received re-education and 7,000 of those were deemed to have committed what he called 'odious crimes' against the people; by which he meant massacres or 'search and destroy' raids to clear whole regions. If they had to be tried in courts of law, he went on, life sentences or death would have been certain. Americans thought of them as political prisoners, we thought of them as criminals: that was the difference, he said.

I thought of Qué – who had never killed anyone in his life. I doubted if Minh had either. Were they 'criminals'? How could they be?

There was one good thing about the reason for their sentence in the camps – Bao Ninh's book has told me of it – that had benefited Minh and Qué, although they didn't know it at the time. They had had *desk jobs*. They had missed at least the nightmare of jungle-fighting and the worst of the appalling casualties that others had had to face for years on end: jets howling on their bombing runs; soldiers blown up by mines and thrown up to the tops of trees; people being killed instantly, or wounded, every bone broken, pleading for death and bleeding to death in agony.

They missed fighting so horrible that, as Bao Ninh, the veteran from

Hanoi – who should know – has written, everyone involved prays to heaven they'll never have to experience any such terror again . . . 'Dying and surviving were separated by a thin line; they were killed one at a time, or all together; they were killed instantly, or were wounded and bled to death in agony; they could live but suffer the nightmares of white blasts which destroyed their souls and stripped their personalities bare.'

At least Minh and Qué had missed all that horror. And to that extent they were lucky.

Bao Ninh wrote a pitiful truth in *The Sorrow of War*. 'Losses can be made good, damage can be repaired and wounds will heal in time. But the psychological scars of the war will remain for ever.' At least for the likes of Minh, Qué and Mme Bong.

Bao Ninh also wrote of the fall of Saigon on 30 April 1975, V-Day. 'It poured with rain. Yes, on that momentous day of total victory, after that terribly hot noon, Saigon had been drenched in rain. After the downpour the sun came out from behind the clouds and the gunsmoke, shining down on the last counter-attack of the South Vietnamese commandos at the airport – as it was beaten off.'

Of course, one can see why to some North Vietnamese troops the entry into Saigon seemed like the end of an era. 'Some said they had been fighting for thirty years, if you included the Japanese and the French. War had been their whole world. So many lives, so many fates. The end of the fighting was like the deflation of an entire landscape, with fields, mountains, rivers collapsing in on themselves.

'It wasn't true that young Vietnamese loved war. Not true at all. If war came they would fight, and fight courageously. But that didn't mean they loved fighting. Not the ordinary people. The recent years of war had brought enough suffering and pain to last them a thousand years.'

*

When Minh left me at the hotel that night I had no idea it was the last time I would see him until he arrived, a bewildered refugee, in Virginia several years later. As for poor, ailing Qué, as I have said, he would not be able to leave Vietnam for another ten years – ten years! – just after I arrived back in a wholly revamped Vietnam, a Vietnam in which at last I was free to hitch a ride on Vu's motorbike to Mme Bong's home for lunch, as I had in the old days.

Just as if nothing had happened at all.

What a miserable time 1985 was in Vietnam. Nothing much in the shops, a few Eastern Bloc tourists shambling about the streets without any hard currency to speak of, and, for the Vietnamese, a great deal of fear.

The revolution was relatively new then. A high-handed government still stuck up posters all over the streets of Ho Chi Minh City advertising 'Freedom Week' and 'Reunification'. One can account for Mr Thai's own high-handedness by those facts and the fact of the tenth anniversary parade to celebrate that final victory of 1975. Triumph can excuse a lot, even a measure of malice. Nevertheless I find what happened to Minh and his family hard to excuse.

One remembers Trotsky's account of the first meeting of the Soviet after the October days of 1917: 'Among their number were completely grey soldiers, shell-shocked as it were by the insurrection, and still hardly in control of their tongues. But they were just the ones who found the words which no orator could find. That was one of the most moving scenes of the revolution, now first feeling its power, feeling the unnumbered masses it has aroused, the colossal tasks, the pride in success, the joyful failing of the heart at the thought of the morrow which is to be more beautiful than today.'

Of course, there are great differences between Vietnam and Soviet Russia; and enormous differences between the nature of the peoples of those two countries. We know now that 'the morrow' in the case of

Soviet Russia was anything but 'beautiful', and the future of Vietnam – although it is much better already (for many Vietnamese at least) – remains to be seen. From the point of view of Mr Thai and others like him, the pride and the reward for suffering were, of course, a vital outcome of the seemingly endless years of struggle. One can understand his malice, of course, while condemning it utterly.

Part Three

LETTERS FROM EXILE

My experience is not fiction. In fact, it changed many aspects of my life.

No's story of his escape from Vietnam (see Appendix I)

Chapter 7

The documents which Mr Long of the Ho Chi Minh City press office handed to me finally in a manila envelope just as I was about to leave Vietnam in 1985 did in the end prove to be vital. Vital, at least, in sending Mme Bong's second son, Minh, into exile with his wife and two boys.

I have found a letter written from the American embassy in Thailand on 8 May 1985, saying:

The American Embassy gives permission for the above persons to come to Bangkok, Thailand, to make application at this Embassy to go to the United States, provided they have a medical examination in Vietnam and an interview by a representative of the United Nations High Commissioner for Refugees (UNHCR). We request the authorities to issue Exit Permits and the necessary documents to leave Vietnam.

An accompanying letter adds the dire words:

Please understand that this letter does not guarantee that you will receive exit permission. Permission to leave Vietnam must be obtained from the Vietnamese authorities over whom we have no control.

The 'above persons' referred to in the first letter are:

Tran Dinh Minh	born 29 January 1945
Tong Thi Kim Ban	born 20 October 1951
Tran Dinh Quoc Bao	born 20 July 1974
Tran Dinh Quoc Viet	born 08 August 1982

Which adds up to: Minh, his wife and his two sons.

It was going to take Minh and his family six more years to get permission to leave Vietnam despite the payment of considerable sums of money to those authorities.

The next thing that happened was a letter from Mme Bong's son-in-law, Ho Trang, in 1985. It came quite out of the blue from America and bore a postscript which read: 'I'm sorry. I don't speak English very well. There are many mistakes in this letter.' But I could understand what he said:

Do you remember my first boy, which you was his godfather (Ho Tran Dien Hoang; born 1966). His life is very hard in VN. He finished high school in 1982 but he can't continue to college because his father [Ho Trang himself] was a high-ranking officer of the Vietnamese Republic Army.

Well, you can help him. I thank you very much. I just received a letter from my wife. She told me that you were recently in VN and saw my family in Saigon. Thanks to God you don't forget them. I think that is miraculous (supernatural).

OK. Now may I tell you about me? I left VN, Sept. 22 1984. After 5 days and nights I cross the ocean in a small boat 9 metres long, 2.4 metres wide, 67 persons. We were rescued by a Spain ship and were brought to Singapore for 3 months, and after that to the Philippines in June 1985. I have to study English 14 weeks before I go to the U.S.A.

and I left the Philippines Refugee processing centre on June 20th, 1985.
I fly then to Maryland (MD) by Boeing 747 of Northwest Orient
Airlines, landing at Baltimore airport. At the airport I was met by my
sponsor, Lt Colonel Frank K Kline, who was senior adviser when I was
Dien Khanh district chief 1971–1973.

> *Ok, I stop here. Write to me soon,*
> *Your friend*
> *Ho Trang*

Ho Trang had married Minh's sister sometime in the 1960s but I
had never met him, except perhaps once, in his district of Dien Khanh
in Nha Trang Province, where he was a very competent District Chief
in the early 1970s. He had won the Bronze Star of the United States
(with 'V' – for valour – device), said an official American citation dated
1 June 1987. The citation has more to it than that, of course. In awarding
this medal to Major Ho Trang, Army of the Republic of Vietnam, for
heroism in connection with military operations against a hostile force,
it goes on:

> Major Ho Trang distinguished himself by heroic action from 30
> November to 1 December 1972 while serving as District Chief,
> Dien Khanh District. On those dates, while accompanying friendly
> forces in contact with the enemy, Major Trang exposed himself
> to intense enemy fire to provide vital support to the combat
> efforts of the friendly unit . . . He demonstrated sound judgment,
> aggressiveness, and initiative while significantly aiding his unit's
> performance . . .

Another citation – accompanying the award of an Army Commenda-
tion Medal – praised him for 'the long and arduous working hours he
put in' and says 'he set an example that inspired his associates to strive

for maximum achievement'. 'Loyalty, initiative, and the will to succeed', those characteristics were all attributed to Ho Trang time and again in the two citations.

And 'Loyalty, initiative and the will to succeed' were exactly what he most needed to gather together his far-flung family and guide it in their new country of residence.

Ho Trang's next letter was dated 17 July 1986 and the address at the top of the page was: 6085 Bellview Drive, # 302 Falls Church, VA 22041. It was written in longhand and the English language was obviously not something Ho Trang had mastered as yet. The letter said:

Dear Gavin Young,

You know about Dien Hoang [Cun] who is my first boy – that you was god-father for him.

Dien Hoang has escaped from VN on 4 June. After 12 hours, he was rescued by a German ship – and took him to Palawan (island of the Philippines). He was very lucky. This ship is Cap Anamur for German and International Medical Association.

Now he lives in Palawan, Philippine First Asylum Centre. For he must wait JVA (Joint Voluntary Agency) who will come to determine where he must go. I think he have a relative that is living in the US, so that he have to go to US with me. But in HCR's Rules depend on the nationality ship, so refugees must go to that nation. However [I think he meant 'therefore'] maybe he must go to Germany. He worry about it. Now what we do? I think you can help me, telephone to American Embassy in Manila and tell them know about the case of my son and request them for my son who go to US with me as soon as possible.

> *Okay, please try and write to me.*
> *With best regards,*
> *Au revoir, Your friend*
> *H.T.*

Shortly after this a letter arrived from Dien Hoang himself (I later knew him better by his nickname 'Cun', meaning 'little dog' in Vietnamese). His letter came from Palawan, as I expected. It was typewritten.

Dear Sir [it said],

I would like to introduce myself to you. My name is Ho Tran Dien Hoang, twenty years old. When I write my uncle's name, I think you will realise who I am.

I am very pleased to send you this letter, sir. My Mother, my grandmother and my uncle have told me that I have an adopted father who is a journalist. Till the date, 30 April 1985, I just knew you are my adopted father when you returned to Vietnam for getting news of the anniversary. Never before in my life have I seen you; and I am happy that I have an adopted father in my mind.

I escaped from Vietnam on 4 May 1986. Fortunately I was rescued by Cap Anamur *on 5 May 1986. After one month on the sea,* Cap Anamur *took us to Palawan Philippines on 4 June 1986. Because of the guarantee of three countries: W. Germany, France and Belgium, it is rather difficult for me to be reunified with my father in US. The US delegation, JVA, came to our camp for interviewing, but all refugees rescued by* Cap Anamur *were out of their list. Till now, I have not been submitted to US Ambassy yet; although I already received the sponsorship from my father. I must wait for US a more long time.*

My uncle aleady received the Letter of Introduction from you. He can not apply for a file yet in ODP at Vietnam because the Vietnamese Government order to stop the ODP. [I had forgotten this.] *Now, there is only one way to escape is to get a small boat directly to the dangerous sea. My Uncle's family, my mother, with my three brothers and, my grandmother* [Mme Bong] *are still in Vietnam. They are very anxious about my situation. I just received my grandmother's letter telling me to write you a letter. So I write to you immediately.*

Finally, I wish you a good health when you are older and older. I

dream that I should meet you in the near future, sir. It is the first time
I write a letter by [sic] English, so please forgive all my mistakes. Please
give me a chance to call you 'Daddy' as my true adopted father.

An adopted son of yours,

· *Cun*

I was in Hong Kong at that moment gathering material for a history
of Cathay Pacific Airways. I called Manila to speak to the United
Nations High Commission for Refugees to find out if Cun (as I already
called him to myself) would be able to come to the capital of the
Philippines for the Christmas holiday. The answer was 'yes'. And so I
booked a seat on an aeroplane to Manila and a double room at the
Manila Hotel and prepared to spend Christmas with my new godson
there.

I remember meeting the plane that brought Cun from Puerto Princesa
in Palawan Island. I had little difficulty in recognizing him as he came
through the exit gate of Manila airport. After all, a Vietnamese is a
Vietnamese is a Vietnamese, as Gertrude Stein might have said. Then
I bundled him into a taxi and told the driver to head for the Manila
Hotel, a rather grand place facing the sea in the old part of Manila
which I think had been General McArthur's headquarters during the
war.

There followed a week or ten days of delightful holiday. Cun is one
of those Vietnamese who like a drink now and again – not all Vietnamese
do – and he enjoyed himself, I think, falling tipsily in love with a little
Filipina girl in a big store I took him to, buying a guitar, eating at a
Vietnamese restaurant I had discovered, and regularly visiting a Spanish
place where a jolly band played flamenco music very loudly. As for
me, I found Cun as delightful to be with as Vietnamese usually are,
particularly as I knew his family and their Hué friends well, and Cun
spoke quite good English. Also, most important, he had a well-
developed sense of humour. At the end of his holiday he returned to

Palawan, as I had guaranteed the United Nations people he would. He was quite happy to go back now that he had established good relations with a sensible girl – American, I think – called Karen in the UNHCR there and was reasonably sure he would get the interview he wanted with JVA quite soon. This interview was the first necessary step on his way to the United States to join his father, Ho Trang. First, though, he would have to spend a short time in a camp in Bataan, not far from Manila on Luzon Island.

The next letter from Cun reached me in Hong Kong in February. It said:

My dearest Daddy,

All the things become happy and true, now. In the afternoon of 14 February I was transferred by the port of Palawan. Many friends of mine saw me off at the port, they were very sad to say goodbye to me and we cried. How could we separate for journey? But I had to go, though many of my new brothers had to stay in the camp. Then the boat sailed at 8.30 p.m., till the early morning of 16 February. We could see our Manila Hotel dimly at the far side. We landed at 10 a.m. and three buses of ICM brought us to the Transit camp where you and I met Mr Giang and his friend when I was in Manila with you. On the way to the Transit camp, the bus stopped at Rizal Park so that we could carry all the blankets from the laundry. How I miss you there! I saw the Manila Hotel, and I was excited with all my memories. I could not imagine I would see it again before April. The bus ran down the avenue, the streets which we walked back to the hotel. I showed to my friends the places and explained for them like a Manila scout. ['Guide', I think he meant.]*

I stayed at the Transit Camp one day; in the morning of 17 February I was transferred by bus again to Bataan. I wondered what will happen to me there. Everything is very strange to me here, all the things has changed absolutely. The life here is harder than in Palawan, and I was so alone here. I wanted to cry for missing my Palawan friends and wondering about my new life.

This morning I got a calling slip for an English knowledge testing tomorrow. It will take me about six months to be here. I was taking a rest before going to see a film about the life in this camp when Miss Karen came suddenly. I was very surprised and happy to see her again. This is a signal from you, is it right, my dearest Daddy? Really, she told me you are anxious for my situation. Daddy, please don't worry so much about me, since I am a man now. The ups and downs of my life have continually made me stronger and stronger. From now on I know that you are in Hong Kong. I will regularly write my letters to you.

Are you well after flying to Hong Kong? Please be careful with your health. I am afraid when ever you get sick. I hope to see you soon, my dearest Daddy, and desire to have your letter soon.

Your son,

Cun

Palawan, 23 Feb. 1987

My dearest English teacher!
(Oh, my dearest Daddy, to be more exactly).

I am so glad to inform you that I was accepted by INS Officer in US Refugee Program on the very morning of the first day of Tet (29 Jan. 87)! How wonderful it was! Daddy, all the things have truely happened to me as your wish – Happy Tet.

Dearest Daddy! How can I tell you my happiness now!?! As you know, Karin said that I could be considered on next April, since I came of age already. On last Monday, JVA came to our camp in order to prepare for INS interview. I believe in Karin and thought that there there was not my name on the list of interviewing this time, so I was very uneventful about that. When I reached to UNHCR office, I saw JVA talking with Mr Nils, of the Canadian Delegation. Suddenly a friend of mine called and told me that I was luckily considered this time, I jumped immediately to the list. In fact, there was a list of Cap Anamur *for prescreening, I was surprised when I did not see my name through up and down of the list. Why? I thought my friend only told me a joke, but he confirmed again that he had just seen my name. I rightway remembered the last time, these had been a list of prescreening as well as INS interviewing of* Cap Anamur, *I anxiously turned to the end of the list . . . Can you guess what is there and how I was at that time? There was my name, really, Daddy, to see INS; I just wanted to shouting a loud for happiness. After awaiting 8 months without any information of my files, the Spring Queen have brought to me the great happiness all at once.*

Then, JVA began working and I was a interpreter for them. I was prescreened by Mrs Marilyn Marcelo on 28 Jan. 87. (She was very, very nice to me, Daddy, she softly asked me about my family. In Tet, I missed my mother so much, and Mrs Marilyn's smiles looked like my mother very much. I told her our story, she remembered what she had told Karin about my cases. She said that afterwards, she'd seen it could be possible to put my name on the list and she has done. INS officer interviewed me on 29 Jan. 87, Daddy it was the first day of Tet. In that morning, I still worked with Mrs Marilyn. When it came my files, I asked for permission to stop working and went into INS Room. I said good morning to INS officer and his Vietnamese interpreters. His interpreters smiled and told her that I was Mrs Marilyn's interpreter. Then she turned to me: 'You must answer directly to him in English!' By God! It was my fateful point that I couldn't make any mistake, I feel tremble. The INS officer began asking very quickly, 10 times quicklier than Mrs Marilyn. But, at that time, I suddenly answered fluently his question about the reason why I had left Viet Nam. Now I cannot understand what helped me to keep calm. He asked me about 10 questions, and I answered easily like I did before the JVA. Finally, he said: 'Good luck, I'll approved your file and I hope to see you in

American.' Then, he glanced at me! Oh, Daddy, I wished I could have fled to the seventh sky!

Dearest Daddy, 'what will be will be', I finally see all my dreams have gradually become true.

I have received your second letter, too and I was very happy and try to read your novel which is very, very difficult for me.

My dearest Daddy, please keep healthy and share the happiness with me. We will talk a lot of things when I meet you.

Your son,

Cun

* My dear English Teacher!

Would you please correct my letter, I try to write without dictionary. So I've got many mistakes. Please, forgive me, Dad . . .

I was of course delighted to hear from Cun that he had been cleared to join his father in the United States. Incidentally, I thanked God that Cun had had the good luck to get to the Philippines – the UNHCR people there (and the Filipinos themselves) seem to have behaved better or more compassionately than in any other Asian country. Perhaps it was that the Filipino government, for all its shortcomings, was more compassionate in a general way.

Bata-an, 20 Feb. 87

My dearest Daddy,

It's my fourth day in new camp. After being confused with many thing, now I have got aqquainted with my new life. Yesterday, I was called for general health examination in the morning. Then, I had a test for English in the afternoon. Thanks to my basic of English knowledge, I was chosen to be an assistant teacher. I will have a week of training on next 23rd before working. At the beginning, I feel empty since I have no duty in the camp; I hope in future my works can make me happier. It takes me about 6 months to be in the camp, it would be a short time if I knew how to use this duration!

Miss Karin told me that she would try to help me to shorten the duration. I was very happy to hear that, but now I wonder that she could not. All the persons here must follow the rule of PRPC, we can not bend the rule, my dearest Daddy!

Are you well, Daddy? The weather hear is rather different than in Palawan. It's colder in the night and hotter in the day, because the camp is located in the valley surrounded by many mountains. Besides us, there are some of Laotians, Cambodians, too. PRPC teaches us how is American life. That means working, taking bus . . . It's very funny that there are many classroom at each neighborhood; but when I live at neighborhood ten, I must go to school at neighborhood 2, 1. Because of the very distant way for working, we must get up early to take the bus on time. On occassions that I am late, I must take the trycicles which are drived by Philippino 'jungers, cowboys', and pay P1. We can not drink beers in the camp. If any policeman see us drink beer, he will put us to be in jail about 1 month, so beer is not sold in the camp.

I will tell you my life when I see you, Daddy! Some are funny, but some are sad. Please answer my letter immediately. I'm very anxious about you.

Your son,
Cun

A number of letters arrived from Cun over the next few months, and one from Minh in Saigon (translated by Cun).

If only Qué could get to Manila, I thought. And as it happened, almost at once Cun wrote me a letter (he had reached Virginia, now) referring to Qué. It went as follows:

Va, 27 Aug. 88

Dearest Daddy,

I would like to wish you'd help your other old Vietnamese friend, Mr Qué.

I have just received from Vietnam his letter asking my father to help him get in to ODP. He has learnt that the Viet Cong Government openly allow the US to accept eleven thousands re-educationers. Based on his background in army before 1975 and six years in the re-education camp, he hoped to reach out of Vietnam legally in the US human program. He sent us his documents – his family's birth certificates, his marriage certificate as well as his release paper and his background. I am very sorry that I have not translated them into English! Many friends of my family ask my father to sponsor for them. In Mr Qué's case, I think that it could be much effective with your help than with my father's. If the US ODP office in Bangkok gave him a letter, LOI (letter of introduction), his family could apply for visa considering in Vietnam. So, dearest daddy, please let me know your opinion as soon as possible. Then, I immediately send you all his documents.

My brother [Ly] and Bao write regularly to me. They hope that they will be transferred to Panathnikhom camp in the end of this year. There, the UN will file their resettlement. The life is hard; but, they can suffer to wait for reuniting us in American. I started my school again yesterday. I also apply for permanent residence card, which I can use for going to Canada or applying for visa to other countries.

Daddy, I wait for your answer letter. My father have me send his best wishes to you. He hope to see you again soon.

Please take care yourself, Daddy. I enclose Mr Qué's family's ID photo.

Yours son,
Cun

Then on 19 April 1989 Ho Trang, faced with an influx of his family members from Vietnam, as well as the possibility of the eventual arrival of Minh and his wife, not to mention Bao and Viet, Minh's two sons, got a friend to write me the following important letter from Falls Church, Virginia.

Dear Gavin,

In this translated letter Ho Trang tells you about the housing problems he's faced with. The lease of the house they're in is coming to an end and he doesn't want to renew the lease as the landlord would not permit any more people living there. And, of course, the family hopes that the boys from the Thai camps will be able to join them in the US before too long. If they move, renting another house both Cun and No might have problems in commuting to college every day.

For the last year Ho Trang had to pay $850 monthly rent, with electricity, gas, water, etc. on top of it comes to $1,100 per month.

When you compare the monthly rent to paying off a mortgage he thinks it would be more sensible to buy a house big enough to accommodate all the family when the rest of them are able to join them. He has the idea of buying a 3–4 bedroomed house, including basement, in Washington – near George Mason College – and people have told him this would cost him $150,000, with a down-payment of $20,000, a monthly repayment of between $1,400–$1,500, which they could manage, over a 30-year period. However, he doesn't have the $20,000 for the down-payment. He wonders whether you would be willing to lend him this amount. He would repay the loan to you with interest. If he himself could not continue to pay the money the children would be repaying it to you. If you think this is not right then they could put your name and Ho Trang's name as joint ownership of the house.

Would you please consider this very seriously and, above all, he asks you not to mention it to Cun or No – he does not want them to know until everything is done.

If you do not wish to lend Ho Trang the money you should forget about this letter and remain their good friend.

Please reply to him at his office address, as given in his letter.

I had seen Ho Trang's little house in Falls Church and it was indeed very small. He was going to need something more spacious, and he was quite right to want to *buy* a bigger one. Thank God, I thought, that this former major and American army medal winner was in charge of this large family's affairs. Perhaps only Ho Trang, a tough and realistic man, could have managed so competently to look after such a large and poverty-stricken family in a strange, if glamorous, country.

Of course, when I was in Bangkok again, I went to the United States embassy and dropped Qué's pictures and documents off there and I also made it clear that I would do what I could in the way of sponsorship. Only in retrospect do I know that it would take Qué's family another seven long years to leave Vietnam for the United States. I didn't know that then. I didn't know anything then. Certainly not that I would be able to go back to a truly 'liberated' Vietnam in 1995, and actually see Qué in Saigon before he left it.

As for Cun's brother Ly and his cousin, little Bao, I tried to see them in their camp in Thailand, but permission was not granted. So I never saw them there and was quite unable to give them the personal encouragement they clearly needed. As Cun said in his letter, 'they had to suffer to wait'.

Suddenly out of the blue came a letter from Vua, who had been responsible all those years ago for introducing me to Minh and so to Mme Bong and her world.

Vua's letter was written from Thailand, from a camp in Panat Nikhorn near Chomburi. Not surprisingly, it, like Vua himself, was very excited:

Dear Gavin,

I'm very happy to inform you the good news we have just received. We have just been accepted, yesterday, to enter the USA by the INS American delegation.

So, I must stay here one month more, then I will fly to Manila next month April, 1988. I think after you finish your book we have a chance to meet together at Philippines. When I arrive Manila, I will write a letter to you at once.

I look very much forward to seeing you,

Sincerely,
Bui Huu Vua

For some reason, I never saw Vua in Hong Kong or Manila.

Vua arrived in the Philippines as he had predicted, on 10 April 1988, and was bussed to Bataan Camp, where Cun had been. Vua wrote from Bataan that he was there with his wife and two daughters who were all well. He sent best wishes.

The next time I saw him was in Virginia, USA, when he paid a visit to Falls Church where Ho Trang had a small house – had rented one, I should say – and Vua came to see me and Ho Trang's family. He was living then, I think, in Philadelphia. Later he went to live permanently in Texas.

The next thing to arrive was a letter from Ly. He wrote from his camp in Thailand which was, I know now, up on the Cambodian border; it was called Banthad. Ly's letter said:

Dear Dad,

How are you getting on? We are fine now.

Last week, we landed a trouble fit. There was a shelling along the Thai–Cambodian border. UNHCR ordered that all of the refugees had to prepare to move.

Fortunately I have been in Khao I Dang Camp for translating. This camp is about 50 km far from Banthad. I asked my doctor to bring Bao here from Banthad. So far we are still in Khao Dang camp.

Maybe next Monday, Bao will be sent back to Banthad and I will be here for working a little longer. I can not know when I will be back to Banthad.

Sorry, Dad. My doctor comes back right now. Next time I'll write to you longer. Good luck to you. I hope to see you soon.

Sincerely yours,
Ho Tran Dien Son
('Ly')

Chapter 8

Cun arrived in Virginia in 1987 and immediately wrote me a letter about his own affairs, telling me how happy he was.

Virginia, 12.08.87

Dearest Daddy,

Finally I have reached to here, Virginia, for being able easily to have your call! How happy I am now!!! It is cheaper and easier for me to write you than to call you, so I can gradually think exactly what I want to say, to describe to you as we have talked together in Manila. But first of all, I would like to apologise you about my late writing, I have to fulfil many formalities at the beginning in US.

How can I tell you now, Daddy?! Virginia, it's a very, very beautiful, dreamful, quiet enough place which I have never imagined before when I was in the camp. I was very excited to fly over the Washing DC at night, the scence below me seemed a lightful, magnificant clay model, so beautiful. Last week I had a chance to take a drive round the Washington DC, the development of the city is suitable with the nature and the old architecture-building. How nice it is!!!

My father took me to report to many officer. I have to apply for welfare, social security card, health medicaid . . . etc . . . I will take the class in Northern Virginia Community College for 2 years. Then, after having enough required-credits, I will transfer to University for 4 more years. It's really a long way, Daddy. The government opens a student loan program, I will apply for it to pay the expenditure. The most important thing now is driver-lisence and the car, and the insurance too; without them, I can not do any thing, just like a handicap.

My brother No is healthy in Palawan and regularly writes letter to us every week. Thanks for the help of Mrs Marylin Marcelo – JCA case worker – I think that his file can be considered on the next month. Then, we will reunify together again on November. Till now, he has not sent me his case number, only: 'Group 103/642 Cap Anamur'. I'll ask him now. Marylin has met and talked with him, she was happy when he spoke English in talking.

Your son,
Cun

Virginia, 25 Aug. 87

Dearest Daddy!

We have just received a letter from my father's bank informing us that your money to my uncle has been transferred in my father's account. I can not say anything to you, Daddy, it's my uncle's responsibility. I have just written him a letter, perhaps my uncle will write directly in French to you. And, of course, as you know, I'd like to say thank you very much first.

Another happy thing which just came to us yesterday is that we were informed to make some final paperwork in sponsoring my brother No – he has been accepted by US as a refugee! How happy we are!!! Tomorrow my father and I go to Migration and Refugee services to complete it in – person. I hope that my brother No can be here next month – or October.

Your son,
Cun

Virginia, 21 Sept. 87

Dearest Daddy,

I have gradually started my life in this US society. I am a janitor in a building every weekday from 2.00 pm to 10.00 pm. My application from the Nova Community College has been approved, so now I am ready to school at the end of this month. The financial assistance of the feuderal gives me $700.00 every quarter. I have not received it yet, so I had to pay $305.00 for my registered – 18 credits. The college financial aid office will give me back the whole Pell.Grant without any deducation. It will be rather difficult for me to arrange my study and my job, nobody can support me to go to school, I must solve it by myself. The most important thing is always the language – English, if I spoke English influantly, I would open any doors easily now.

My father now is a maintenance of an elementary school with the salary about $750.00 a month. He goes to work from 2.30 pm until 1.15 a.m. With his language trouble, he can not be sent by any public office in electronic technician. He does not want to work with private company because of his oldage. However, everything is better than in Vietnam. He has taught me how to drive a car, I must get an instruction-driver license. Next November, I can be your driver to visit Washington, DC, Daddy.

My uncle has received our telegram of your gift, we have to wait for his letter. Whenever we received his order, I'll send it to him completely in future, he will write directly to you, but he will write my name as the receiver on his envelope in order to avoid the government censorship. So, please read it, it's for you. My grandmother lives healthly with my uncle's family in Sai Gon, she is there.

There are only two more months for my brother No in the camp, we are eagerly to reunify, but we have to follow US program. He regularly writes letters to us. If there is no trouble we are planning to live together in the same room to save our money. I had lived hardly in Vietnam as well as in the refugee camp, so now I can bear anything.

Please don't worry much about me, Daddy, it will take me, of course, a long time to find out some close friend as I had in Vietnam and in the camp. From the time which we have been out of our country, the loneliness is an unusual enemy readily to infiltrate our heart any time. We have to struggle at any time.

Daddy, please don't worry much about me, please take care of yourself.

Your son,

Cun

Va., 12 Nov. 87

Dearest Daddy,

I just received my uncle's letter; so I translated and send it to you now. My brother Khanh [that is: No] will reach here on next Wednesday, 18th, we were informed last week. Yesterday, it was the first time I saw the snow flurrying around. It's rather interesting, but really dangerous for me to drive. My college is closed today so I have to thank to the snow for an acidentual holiday.

My studying in College is going well, I have easily studied in Maths and English, too. However, I am an janitor in a building in Springfield, far away from my house, about 7 miles. I work from 6 p.m. to 9.30 p.m. Sometimes, I feel tired out, but when I see my father who works from 6 a.m. to 11 p.m. every weekday, I feel that I have to recover myself. My father has worked so much, but it's still not enough to take my family out of regular troubles.

And how are you now, Daddy? I think that you are in Hongkong to avoid the cold weather in England. I am sorry that you cannot visit Manila again to see my brother. However it saves your money. Please write me when you are really free.

Your son

Cun

Va., 22 Dec. 87

Dearest Daddy!

One year passed quickly that I am here far from Manila Hotel! I am very sorry not to write you regularly because of the busy life in this country. You may now be in Hong Kong, I guess, to avoid the London terrible winter. Are you well, Daddy? I took the final exam on last week, so now I am off untill 11 January. Every night I drive my brother, No, to work together as janitors about 7 miles from home. It's rather funny that when I think I have ever lived with you in the best hotel of the Philippines with a thousands persons ready to serve us! And now, the reality is different, I am only a normal person like other Vietnamese refugees. I am very interesting in the ups and downs of myself, do you feel that Daddy?

I have sent my uncle's letter to you. His family, my grandmother and my mother still live together in Saigon. We are planning for one more my brother, Hoa, to escape in the next year. In the last letter, my mother wrote that a local policeman went to our house to ask my uncle about you, the relationship between our family and you. Although there are a lot of those policies, the communist government has still kept closely his attentions on people.

Dearest Daddy, I wish you in very good health on this Christmas. My father dare not write you because of his limit knowledge in English, he's afraid. He'd like to send you the best wishes. We all hope to see you on next April.

Always your son,
Cun

The next letter to arrive came from Minh. Written in Saigon, the first phrase of it was in French and the rest in English which is a language of which at that time Minh did not know a word. So the letter had been written for him, I presume. Never mind; it was a relief to hear from him in any language.

Saigon, 08 Oct. 87

Mon très cher Gavin,

My family and I have happily received your gift which you send to help us. My wife and Viet were very excited to your sympathy reserving for us. Perhaps, I will send you a picture of all our family in my next letter. You will see how old my children have grown when if compare them with the year 85.

My mother left Hué to Saigon to live with us. She's now older and older, so she needs to be taken care by us. She has written you a letter.

All my family would like to send you our best wishes,

Sincerely yours
Tran Dinh Minh & Kim Ban [his wife]

Va., 19 Nov. 87

Dearest Daddy,

My father and I were very surprised to see his balance account after he had withdrawn some money! We did not believe it true and thought that it was a mistake of machine. Few days later, my father received the information from the bank telling us it is really of you. I wonderred what you wanted to do for and I guessed certainly that I would have your letter soon. In fact, I receive your letter today; after I sent my uncle's letter to you few days ago.

Dearest Daddy, I am so clumsy to describe my thoughts to you. As you know, money is really needed anywhere, but, according to me, the value of a man is the way how he face the life to struggle. After living hardly in the communist life, I know exactly that the ability to struggle life helps me to survive. Daddy, yes, I know I am too poor now, yes, I know sometimes I feel lonely, but I try to solve my problems by working, by keeping a friend who has lived with me in Bataan sharing a room in our rent house. Please, don't worry so much about me since besides me, there is my father always. American is our new land, we know that we must begin our new life with our empty hands and our brains.

And our future result is based on our trying now. It is not too easy for you to earn money, nor for me.

Last night, we were happy to pick up my brother No at Washington National Airport. He is taller than the last time I saw him, and blacker. Now, with a long trip, he seems weak and tired. I will looking for a high school so that he can attend without losing time. I'll send you some pictures, at the airport and in our room.

The winter is coming here, weather is colder but, I think it's not terrible like the weather in London. My first quarter will be ended on 18 December. I have good grades in Maths and English, so it encourages me a lot in studying.

Dearest Daddy, you and I now are small parts in a running tremendous machine of life. I wish that you know what I think. I try to do what I think makes you proud of – a millionaire in 1997!!! Oh! Daddy, I only try although I know that I can not. How are you planning to purnish me if I can not? Daddy, to make me a dog in the next life?

Your son,

Cun

But a year later another letter came from Minh, this one sounding anguished in the extreme. It had to do with the fate of Ly and Minh's son Bao, who had reached Thailand after various terrible experiences and then seemed to have disappeared between camps.

This time the letter was in French:

My dear Gavin,

I am very concerned about the fate of my son and his cousin. They are called Bao, born the 20 July 1974 at Hué, and Son, born the 28 March 1968 at Hué. They arrived in Thailand on 20 January 1988 and were shut up in the refugee camp called Laemgop, Thailand.

From that moment until now I have had no news of them at all. Normally Son and Bao should have been moved from Laemgop to

another refugee camp which is called Panat Nikhorn – the camp in
which Vua and his family were put – but unfortunately this could not be
realized because orders from Bangkok insisted on other arrangements.

My wife has wept a great deal and she cannot sleep at night for
worrying about them, about these brave small boys . . .

Your friend,
Tran Dinh Minh

I could do nothing owing to the wretched ban imposed by the Thai
government on foreigners wishing to visit refugee camps. Now I know
that the two boys had been moved to Banthad camp near the Cambodian
border. There Bao was outrageously maltreated by the Thai soldiers –
on one occasion being pushed into an echoing metal barrel which the
soldiers excitedly kicked down the road in order to make the experience
even more confusing and frightening. Poor little Bao – only twelve or
thirteen – was stark naked at the time. There was a good deal of this
sort of thing. Nobody did anything to stop it – not the Thai officers,
nor the Red Cross personnel, not even the UNHCR people.

Still, Bao and Ly were tough, and they survived. I saw them not too
much later in New York when they came up to see me there from
Virginia with Cun and No. I took all of them to dinner and (perhaps
ill-advisedly) to see a Broadway musical called *City of Angels* which
they sat through with expressions on their faces of extreme bafflement.
The main thing was, though, that Ly and Bao had survived their escape
psychologically as well as physically. Ly is now studying to be a doctor
and Bao, who plans to become a pharmacist, is still at college.

Md, 1/24/90

Dearest Daddy,

Good new, Daddy, my uncle Minh will fly to Bangkok on 22nd of
February 1991 with his family. I don't know exactly when they arrive
in US. They may stay at Bangkok at least a week for processing paper

and checking their health again. On the other hand, my mom will be interviewed on the day after they leave Vietnam. Hopefully she will join us on the summer.

No will go to Norway for 3 weeks in Marine Corp. on 26th of Feb. It interupts his semester a little.

I moved to Maryland yesterday. I share a room with $250 a month, about 15' to my school. Spring Semester has begun, and I hope I'll do better in this semester.

Take care of yourself, Dad.

Your son,
Cun

Even more recently Minh finally came to America. He was accepted and flew to Bangkok in 1990. Cun wrote to me about it all. So it was really fortunate that Ho Trang had bought that big house in Fairfax; there was just enough room for all of them to squeeze into it. Meanwhile No had joined the US Marine Corps, and – thanks to the tough training at Boot Camp – had grown to an enormous size. (I think No's choosing to join up was connected with his school fees; the marines paid something towards them.)

The worst news comes next. A letter from Minh, in English this time, talked about Bao and Viet, his sons, but then it gave me a dire warning about Ho Trang's health. This took me completely by surprise; I had no idea there was anything seriously wrong with him. 'I'm afraid Ho Trang will [be] gone to another world,' said Minh. And I deeply regret to have to say he was absolutely right.

October 4/94

Dear my friend,
This is Minh. How's about you.
Bao is a fresman, the first year first step in George Mason University,

he must be to work there about two year, if he can past there after two years, he can transfer to Virginia Medical School, to continue his studies. Bao always talk with you, he want to become a pharmacist.

Viet is leaving from Elementary school, he takes place at an Middle School for 7 grades in this years and 8 grades in next year, after that, he will be enter in a high-school from 9 grades to 12 grade, the way is so far . . . ? But now, Viet is so tall and you did not recongnie him –

An important thing, I want to announce to you, it's Ho Trang very, very sick, may be when you receive my letter, everything is too late, I am afraid. Ho Trang will gone to another world.

I'm so much hurry, so please take care and don't forget all my family we missed you so much.

Always love,
Minh

Poor Ho Trang's death was a disaster. I missed him terribly the next time I visited my Vietnamese friends in Virginia.

Yet there was a curious aftermath.

On nearly my last day in Fairfax, I was leaving Minh's house with a much-subdued Qué and in doing so met by chance Ho Trang's widow, that is Minh's sister, on the point of closing the door of her own house behind her.

'Would you like to come with me?' she asked us. 'I'm going to the pagoda to visit Ho Trang's ashes. It's not far.'

I had wondered where Ho Trang's tomb was, but I hadn't liked to ask. In any case, I was surprised to hear there was such a thing as a pagoda anywhere near Fairfax. We were, after all, deep in the Virginian countryside. You couldn't, I would have thought, expect to find a pagoda hereabouts.

We clambered into the little Japanese car and she drove off, following a sign that said 'Manasses'. Manasses, or Bull Run, was the name of two extremely bloody battles in the American Civil War. That made it somehow even less likely to be the site of a Buddhist temple: but that was where we headed.

It took about half an hour to get to the straggling copse in which the pagoda was situated. It was like no pagoda I had ever seen in Vietnam or Thailand. We turned to the right down a short driveway and came to a couple of wooden single-storeyed houses; unpretentious shacks. There seemed to be nobody about and the first door we came to was locked. It was lucky at that moment a car turned in after us and a man and a woman who might have been Vietnamese got out of it. The man smiled at us and said something and quickly unlocked the door of the house we had tried to open, and let us in. They both walked to the second house, walked into it, closed the door behind them, and disappeared. It was evidently where they lived. Perhaps the man was a monk, or the guardian of the temple. At any rate, the first house was obviously the pagoda in question. It was quite bare except that its walls were covered with plaques with Vietnamese names on them and dates: plaques to dead refugees. One wall was completely taken up with a large Buddhist shrine, with flowers and dishes of fruit offerings, and brass candlesticks, and of course above all a large statue of Buddha in gold leaf.

Thrusting her hand behind a cloth that covered the shrine, Mme Ho Trang pulled out a box and began tenderly to wipe it. This clearly was the box that contained Ho Trang's ashes. She gently laid it on the shrine before pointing to a plaque with Ho Trang's portrait on it. In the photograph I was faintly surprised to see he was wearing glasses. We lit joss-sticks and put them, as custom dictates, in pots placed on the shrine to receive them. And Qué and I stood waiting while she fell to her knees and began to pray, holding her hands, palms together, in front of her face.

'I miss him so much,' she murmured. 'So much.'

There was passion and anguish in those words and I expected to see tears running down her cheeks. But when she replaced the box of ashes behind the altar cloth (what else can I call it?) she was dry-eyed and quite composed.

Then she calmly led Qué and me towards the door and, locking it behind her, made her way in stony silence, but with the utmost decorum, to the car. I held her door open for her, and she stepped in quite without fuss and in a moment drove us on to the high road, as if this visit had been nothing out of the ordinary, as if it was something she did every day. I think – I *like* to think – she felt at peace. 'Manasses' said a sign along the road through the saplings, and 'Bull Run' said another.

In the silence I thought what a good thing it was that Ho Trang and Minh's sister had met in Fairfax together at last, and that he had bought the house, and that now she was able to bring up their four boys in a house next door to Minh, *his* wife and their two sons.

The only thing was that Vietnam was thousands of miles away, and Mme Bong was still in Saigon, going blinder and deafer. Minh and his sons and his wife – all of them were *Viet Kieu* – and I doubted if that fact would ever change. They were Americans, and Americans had driven them here, and had obliged Ho Trang to be buried in a pagoda in of all places Bull Run, Virginia. Perhaps his wife would eventually join him there, and Minh and Minh's wife. Was it fair? Wasn't that character in the Joseph Conrad novel right who sadly noted that 'the great Republic's collective temperament is lawless'.

'I miss him so much,' Ho Trang's widow had said in a shaking voice. And she had repeated it: 'I miss him so much.' Had Mme Bong said the same thing over the tomb of Van at Nui Binh? How many Vietnamese mothers and widows have said that?

Ho Trang died of liver cancer in 1994 in considerable pain. But at least he died in the house he had bought in Fairfax, surrounded by his family: his wife and his four sons, Cun, Ly, No and Hoa. I suppose it might have been worse. He might have died alone, separated by thousands of miles from his kith and kin with his family stranded in Vietnam.

Those medals showed the kind of man he was. I wondered how the family would get on without him.

I visited Fairfax, Virginia, again of course – they still lived there, although Minh had decided to move his wife and two sons to a pleasant rented house nearby. The last time I was there it was a holiday weekend and they were all at home and ebullient as ever. I was relieved to find Cun looking better than I had imagined he would; recently he had become a 'drop-out' at school. He had begun to look thin and weak, and I feared that his health, like his father's, might be giving out. He had come to America with such high hopes, poor Cun; he could hardly help being disappointed in himself. He had, I believe, run into debt and had been forced to give up studying. He was working full-time for the post office now, delivering the mail in a van, at all hours of day and night. That hard, regular work seemed to be doing him good.

By now, it was nearly thirty years since my first meeting in Hué with Minh and Vua. Now one of them was in Fairfax, Virginia; the other was in Texas. And Ho Trang, the strongest character I think I have ever met, the man with 'the will to succeed' who had steered his family through the ultimate disaster of escape and exile, had died. He had died, but he had gathered his wife, her brother, and all his four sons around him in his house and they owned it now. That was quite an achievement. It deserved another medal, an important one at that.

Part Four

GOING BACK

Yes: I have re-entered your olden haunts at last;
Through the years, through the dead scenes I have tracked you . . .

*

. . . all's closed now, despite Time's derision.

Thomas Hardy: 'After a Journey'

Chapter 9

I flew into Hanoi airport in 1995, ten years after my first postwar visit, and this time I was prepared for the worst. After the trauma of 1985 how could I believe that there had been a real transformation in Vietnamese official attitudes to foreigners, particularly to former Western journalists like myself?

I was utterly wrong. Things *had* changed – and greatly for the better.

For a start, I arrived at the airport at about 12.45 p.m. and by three o'clock was sitting with my Vietnamtourism guide on a bench by Hanoi's West Lake having checked into the Saigon Hotel. To my surprise there had been no trouble at all at the immigration counter and Mr Nguyen Van Chuong was a youngish, well-dressed guide of impeccable politeness whose breath, unlike Mr Thai's, was as fresh as pure air. He had a round, cheerful face, totally lacking in guile; a face one could trust.

A thick mist rose from the surface of the West Lake giving it an otherworldly look, and a peaceful, holiday feeling came over me which never left me as long as I was in Vietnam. It was a bit like coming home. When I asked Mr Chuong if it was true that I was not allowed by law to take notes in public or any photographs at all (I had read that in some guidebook in Bangkok), he laughed in a genuinely open fashion and said, 'Why shouldn't you take notes and photographs? Of course,' he smiled, 'I'd rather you didn't take pictures of any Air Force planes you may see about the place. But other than that, you are free, Mr Young, to do what you like.'

When he said that, I understood that things really had changed. And later the months I spent in Vietnam proved what he said was nothing but the truth. Mr Chuong was as unlike Mr Thai Reading as anyone could be. I sighed with relief and out of the corner of my eye I saw Mr Chuong glance at me with interest and – I think – understanding. 'Yes,' he said, with another fleeting smile, and then, dropping his eyes, added, 'Things *have* changed.'

I remembered too well my arrival ten years before; the smears of Bovril mixed with Gillette shaving soap on the hotel sheets; the way the hotel cashier added fictitious items on to my bill; the corrupt official in the Press Centre who tried to double the air fare on my ticket to Ho Chi Minh City; the foreign diplomats – the ambassador so naïvely impressed with smiling pilgrims at a pagoda, the odd Soviet Bloc attachés who looked manly enough but wore skirts and so were probably women, the West German ambassador who had found rats in his deep freeze. I remembered, too, the unsmiling faces and the empty shops.

'When were you last here, Mr Young?'

'Exactly ten years ago, Mr Chuong.'

'Oh, well,' he said, nodding his head emphatically. 'Things have certainly changed since then.'

I had dutifully followed Mr Thai on an obligatory visit to the mausoleum which houses the mummified body of Ho Chi Minh. He took me there because it was his duty. This time I volunteered to go there. Now that there was no need to I wanted to go to please Mr Chuong. Not that he seemed too keen when once we got there and had to join the long, slow queue. The real 'Uncle Ho' only surfaced in my consciousness – and I think in his – when we wandered into the simple bamboo house in which Ho had lived from 1958 to 1969, situated opposite the mausoleum and altogether a much more human affair. The house was tiny and spartan among sinuous palms and tall leafy trees, and looked over a fish pond in which you could see the fishes' vague shapes gliding between the lotus petals.

Un homme pur comme Lucifer – even a South Vietnamese opponent of Ho's had said that of him. To Graham Greene he had given an impression of simplicity and candour, sitting there sipping tea in khaki drill with thick dark woollen socks falling over his ankles. 'Everything had contributed: a merchant ship, the kitchens of the Carlton Grill, a photographer's studio in Paris, a British prison in Hong Kong as well as Moscow in the hopeful spring days of the Revolution, the company of Borodin in China . . .' He spoke an easy, colloquial English, and 'when he put on his glasses to read a paper, bending down a little and sideways, shifting his English cigarette in long, bony, graceful fingers, the eyes twinkling at some memory I had stirred, I was reminded of a Mr Chips, wise, kind, just (if one could accept the school rules as just), prepared to inflict sharp punishment without undue remorse (and punishment in this adult school has lasting effects), capable of inspiring love.' I regretted, said Greene, 'I was too old to accept the rules or believe what the school taught.'

He got up to return to work (the National Assembly was meeting next day), said Greene, 'and his socks flapped as he waved back at me from the doorway, telling me not to hurry . . . to have another cup of tea . . . I could imagine them flapping all across the school quad, and I could understand the loyalty of his pupils.'

The old Confucian pagoda in Hanoi contained a series of carvings of tortoises – which mean 'longevity' and 'wisdom'. In one niche a crane stood on a tortoise's back, and this meant Longevity was allied with Happiness.

'Remember, Mr Chuong,' I said sententiously, 'longevity and happiness do not necessarily go together.'

'What is that?'

'Old age and happiness are not necessarily the same thing.'

'I suppose not.'

'Are you happy, Chuong?'

He nodded. 'I am happy because I missed the war.'

'You've every right to be glad of that. And I suppose you're too young to remember much of it at all?' I couldn't imagine having such a conversation with Mr Thai.

'I remember nothing of it. I was five years old when it ended.'

'Just think, if the French and Ho Chi Minh had come to an agreement in 1945, what misery would have been avoided. The whole American war, for a start. How many Vietnamese do you think died in the war, Chuong?'

He smiled. 'No one could count that many.'

Here we were, Chuong and I, reading a plaque that said the American Express Company had 'been happy to finance, under a reconciliation agreement' the restoration of the old Confucian pagoda in central Hanoi. The turtles looked at us, superciliously.

Mr Chuong looked at me and asked, 'Have you ever eaten dog meat?'

'I don't really know,' I said. 'I might have done, if no one told me what it was.'

Due to exports to China, there might be a shortage of good dogs to eat (Mr Chuong had told me sadly that that was the case) but, unlike ten years ago, the shops were full of everything else. The streets were even full of smiling faces, which was something I had only previously associated with Saigon. I had to admit, too, that Hanoi has a mysterious charm. Perhaps because it is much smaller than Saigon, it is very beautiful; I hadn't noticed before the handsome French colonial build-ings and the avenues of flame trees, Hanoi's parks and lakes with their tiny pagodas magically perched on islands in the middle of the misty water. Now I even had time to notice the good restaurants and the Vietnamese men in khaki solar topees and some of the three or four bars – particularly one called Gustave's which is managed by a tall big-nosed Frenchman whom I called '*mon Général*' because he looks a little like a genial Charles de Gaulle, and his wife, a good-looking and diminutive Franco-Vietnamese, who naturally to me became '*Tante Yvonne*'.

One day I drove towards the mouth of the Red River delta beyond Haiphong. I had heard of the beauty of Ha Long Bay and the limestone rocks that punctuated the sea for many kilometres along the coast. It had become a famous tourist trap.

The drive took four hours over a difficult, bumpy road which was now and again crossed by a railway line, usually at an awkward angle and often on an embankment; at such points, traffic halted and built up for perhaps half an hour at a time. Once we pulled up at a ferry crossing, and the ancient, rusty ferry boat crept across a wide canal which reminded me of the canal at Phat Diem at the southern side of the delta across which, I had read, French Legionnaires had had to pole their way in a punt with difficulty since the water was full of dead Vietnamese civilians, 'like a stew with too much meat'.

That had been way back in the early fifties, at a time when the Viet Minh had almost beaten the French. They had finally done so in 1954 when the North Vietnamese commander, General Vo Nguyen Giap, forced the mass surrender of the French forces at Dien Bien Phu far away near the border of Laos to the west of where we were now. Who here would remember now the French planes swooping down over the Red River to fire a burst from their cannons and blow apart sampans in a shower of sparks; sampans which, for all anyone knew, might have been home to nobody more dangerous than a poor fisherman and his wife?

The Suoi Mo Hotel at Ha Long probably dated from the 1970s or 1980s, the Soviet age of Vietnam's postwar period; it was not very good at $40 a night, though cheap by Saigon standards, and it still has 'Regulations for Guests' in Russian in a prominent place by each door.

The hotel was inundated when I got there by Korean and Taiwanese tourists – although the Taiwanese after one night were replaced by a busload of Singaporeans. The Singaporeans spent a lot of their time raucously shouting at each other – it seemed the way in which they preferred to communicate. Strange; I have spent a good bit of time in Singapore in the past thirty years, but I have never noticed that the inhabitants of that rugged little island are particularly noisy in their own habitat. Here in Ha Long, like so many Macbeths, the Singaporean Chinese tourists, oblivious to anyone else, succeeded in murdering everybody's sleep.

Luckily it is the daytime that counts in Ha Long – that is the time to get out on the sea among those amazing crags that emerge dramatically from it, like scaly teeth, as they do in Krabi in Thailand, though they are smaller in size.

The thing to do is to spend a day cruising on a simple motorboat with a crew of two round these extraordinary rocks. There are plenty of boats for hire. Some rocks are shaped like bowler or top hats, some are like great Roman noses thrusting up from the water; in every direction thousands of them run off into the distance while eagles float overhead and vegetation covers their towering stone heads and sides like wild, disordered drapery. One or two of the bigger rocks have deep caves which one can climb up into, and a small fleet of fishing vessels skim about among crags shaped like fighting cocks or others with fluted sides like gigantic church organs surrounded by sea. As we drew away from the pier a tiny skiff, crewed by a small girl and her diminutive brother, came alongside and sold us shrimps and crabs that were so fresh that they still wriggled in a bowl of sea water, and lunch that day consisted of those shrimps and crabs, broken open in our fingers, and cold beer. It was quite enough. The breeze remained fresh throughout the day, and at sunset the western sky turned a brilliant red colour, like the loom of a city on fire.

*

Even so, after the four hours' drive back to Hanoi, I was glad to see Gustave's Bar again and the *Général* and *Tante Yvonne*, and when I had scrambled up to their second floor for dinner (French cuisine, for a change), I came down to find a small Vietnamese jazz band playing in the bar. The pianist bashed away quite expertly. He knew all about the American jazz pianists Oscar Peterson and Teddy Wilson, who had once been my friends, and without benefit of a professional teacher had taught himself on a ramshackle piano at home by listening to old cracked 78-records. Like Mr Chuong, he remembered nothing of the war. He liked jazz and pianos. Was there nothing these Vietnamese couldn't do?

That question resurfaced when Mr Chuong took me on my last night in Hanoi (I was going to Saigon the next day) to see the Water Puppet show in which expert Vietnamese puppeteers miraculously manipulate their dolls on the surface of a water tank.

Hanoi, renewed, had changed itself unrecognizably – and, in turn, it had changed my appreciation of Vietnam.

Uncle Ho sleeps embalmed in his hideous mausoleum, but in spirit he slumbers on in the peaceful garden-house opposite. The rice fields on either side of the road from the airport spread out like a gleaming emerald carpet, and men and women stoop over the paddy like coloured markers on a map.

I, like Greene, regretted I was too old to accept the rules of Uncle Ho's school or to believe what it taught. The blinkered communists who ruled in Hanoi after 1975 reduced the country to penury. They expelled my friends from Hué so that instead of using their brains to build up their own country (which is all they wanted to do) they are far away, exiles in a strange land, trying to make the best of it.

Yet there was something else Greene had remarked on with which I could agree, particularly when I saw those men and women stooping in the paddy fields.

We talk so glibly of the threat to the individual, but the anonymous peasant has never been treated like an individual before. Unless a priest, no one before the Commissar has approached him, has troubled to ask him questions, or spent time in teaching him.

Of course the story is not ended yet; perhaps it has only just begun.

'Four million Vietnamese died in the war. Fifty-eight thousand Americans, too,' said Mr Chuong sadly, seeing me off to Saigon. Then he cheered up and added with a ring of pride in his voice, 'Vietnam is a great exporter of rice. Perhaps the third in the world after America and Thailand.'

Plus ça change, I thought. In any case I was so impressed by this peaceful garden-house that I vowed to return to it.

But soon I was in the Vietnamese Airlines Airbus – this time with overhead lockers and seatbelts – flying to Saigon where I knew Mme Bong would be waiting for me.

Chapter 10

It was strange – and thrilling – to be back in Saigon again, a place in which I had spent so much time twenty to thirty years before. At first it seemed not to have changed – and yet, of course, it had changed a great deal. Like a ghost, one had to find one's way through a jungle of new houses and altered rooms realizing, as someone has said, that concrete and steel can proliferate like vegetation.

My new hotel – the Asian – was in a most familiar neighbourhood – just behind the old Continental Hotel (which had been considerably smartened up) in what thirty years ago had been called Tu Do Street and before that (under the French) rue Catinat. Now it had become Dong Khoi Street. The Asian Hotel, with its automatic doors and bonsai trees in pots in the lobby, faced the offices of the Saigon Tourist Service across the street, a handsome pale green building with an old French colonial-style façade which may have been there before but which I can't remember. On either side of it were the original old crumbling blocks of flats with red-tiled roofs, all newly painted, and below them was the daily roaring bedlam of motorbikes and cyclos and only rarely the odd car or taxi. There were no traffic jams in Saigon as yet – although they were gloomily predicted: the place would become another Bangkok, said knowing foreigners.

One thing was missing – for which one was extremely glad: the wartime thudding of American helicopter engines overhead, the flashes of gunfire around the city's horizon at night, and the distant drumming of the guns out towards Bien Hoa. All these things were mercifully absent. When Mme Bong's grandson Vu urged me to hop on the back of his old motorbike and be driven to the suburb of the city to the little house she lived in now, we had to wobble through the bicycles and Hondas to the theatre in front of the Caravelle Hotel (a new star called Elviscong was performing at the theatre, I noticed), turning left there, and left again at Hai Ba Trung Street.

The Caravelle was advertising the opening of a Japanese restaurant on its top floor – the hotel indeed seemed to have been taken over by the Japanese – and I wondered if the old bar named after the French singer, Juliette Gréco, was still there.

I remembered as if it were yesterday the shooting that had broken out just outside the Caravelle's glass doors early one morning when I was staying there. Running into the street with other journalists, I saw an amazing sight: a swiftly growing horde of American military police in bulletproof jackets was blasting away at something or someone up the street: whatever it was was invisible to us. From the other end of the street answering – or at least what appeared to be answering – shots rang out, although, strangely, no bullets seemed to be coming our way. Minute after minute the number of military policemen grew; they came in jeeps and military trucks, piling out in front of the hotel, yelling orders to each other and cocking their automatic weapons excitedly. The shooting and the yelling continued, getting louder. I crept up behind the front line and peered up the street. All I could see was a shoddy civilian truck stopped in the middle of it about halfway between us and the far end.

The shooting stopped suddenly, and we approached the truck cautiously in a strange silence. It was riddled with bullets. Inside the open back of it ten Vietnamese workers were sprawled. They were all dead. They were middle-aged or old men and women, harmless civilians. They looked as if they had been on their way to work. A few conical hats lay where they had fallen. There was no sign of any weapon.

An officer, as young as Alden Pyle though, unlike Pyle, he had no crewcut, said, 'Oh well, ten less to worry about.'

Only *ten*, after all those bullets?

I wanted to shout at him that suffering is not increased or diminished by numbers. If I had been Fowler in *The Quiet American*, I might have added, 'Perhaps it would make you happier to say they died for democracy.' But it was too late. What good was it to argue with him? He was young. And shaken no doubt by an uneasy sense of his own vulnerability, and possibly by guilt as well.

At an official briefing later that day, an embassy spokesman said something about it having been a tragic mistake. So we journalists had to be content with that.

Now Vu accelerated his ancient motorbike past the very spot on which all those years ago the workers' truck had stalled.

It must have been quite soon after that incident of the workers in the truck that I moved from the Caravelle to the Royal Hotel not far away, on the corner of Nguyen Hué and Nguyen Thiep streets. The Royal was an unpretentious, slightly crumbling little place on three floors, and it was run by a tough, cynical Corsican ex-soldier called Jean Ottavj and his Vietnamese wife. M. Ottavj had a face like a gentle Punchinello (though he had no hunchback), a face as crevassed and gnarled as a map of the Central Highlands of Vietnam. He smoked opium steadily ('fifteen or sixteen pipes a day, *monsieur*'), was devoted to his tiny wife, and had left the French army sometime after the First World War. He had a seemingly unending fund of stories concerning mystical encounters he claimed to have had with such necromancers as the long-dead Count de St Germain, and he read and firmly believed in Nostradamus's daily predictions.

M. Ottavj had spent most of his life in Saigon, which he loved. He told me the French could have stayed if they'd played their cards differently. 'If the French had judged the Vietnamese better,' he used to say unregretfully, 'their army would probably be here today.'

As it was, the Americans were there. Frequently, outside his hotel door, American military police confronted a struggling group of drunken GIs in a gutter strewn with broken glass. At such moments, M. Ottavj would only momentarily break off a story about the Count de St Germain to murmur indifferently, '*Ça arrive . . . ça arrive.*' One expected him to add, '*Plus ça change . . .*' After decades of invasions, riots and the sound of *someone's* artillery booming across the river, he remained kind, and monumentally resigned. To welcome the Americans he had prudently planted a few chattering Vietnamese girls in his old bar ('Call me Curly,' squeaked one of them in an American accent) and extended his restaurant. A number of journalists ate there, including myself. M. Ottavj's *soupe pistou* and his Algerian *vin du patron* (the bottles were distinguished by their day of bottling from special tankers in the port rather than by any year) were much prized.

M. Ottavj's favourite companion when it came to going down to the opium parlour he preferred was a Mr Yeong, an elderly Chinese of extreme emaciation. Mr Yeong – the smoker of heaven knew how many pipes over how many years – had the sunken cheeks and the baby wrists that opium gives you after a long period of indulgence. His voice was a reedy whisper; it could barely be heard. By comparison, M. Ottavj, nearly seventy and of a certain fragility himself, seemed almost like a strapping sergeant major; he towered over Mr Yeong. They were devoted friends. Mr Yeong died (faded away, perhaps I should say), sometime before M. Ottavj, and Ottavj himself died in Saigon shortly after his seventieth birthday party, which was a riotous affair, celebrated in his hotel restaurant. He died in fact just soon enough to be spared the sight of the entry into Saigon of North Vietnamese troops.

The Royal is still there. But it is no longer an hotel and no longer called the Royal. It is a smartish fast food bar called, I think, the Ciao

Bar, very popular with young Vietnamese prostitutes and the hairy European backpackers in shorts and long locks with whom Vietnam today is saturated.

A few doors down Nguyen Thiep Street, however, is a French bar and restaurant called Augustin, good, friendly and cheap. It is nothing like Jean Ottavj's place, but at least an old barman there remembers Jean Ottavj and the Royal.

As it happened, the war came suddenly and unexpectedly back to me the other day as I sat on a bar stool at Augustin, drinking a vermouth-cassis before lunch.

I had my back to the glass doors of the restaurant so I did not see a Vietnamese worker entering to remove two large Calor Gas canisters. Nor did I see him attempt to leave, for if I had done so I would not have jumped from my stool believing that a bomb had gone off in the street. BOOM! What happened, I learned later, was that the man, laden with the two heavy gas canisters, had not seen the thick glass of the door and had walked straight through it. The noise was shattering. It was exactly as if a very large bomb had exploded up the road – just outside M. Ottavj's Royal Hotel, in fact. Glass – thick shards of it – lay everywhere, inside the restaurant and outside on the pavement. People at the bar near me and others already seated in the restaurant, had leapt to their feet, fearing the worst. I drank my drink and ordered another. It was like old times. I could see the ghost of M. Ottavj, pursing and unpursing his lips, murmuring, '*Oh, ça arrive . . . ça arrive, Monsieur Young.*'

As usual, I thought he was going to add, '*Plus ça change . . .*' I had walked him home from his opium parlour one night through streets still tangy from the tear gas that had broken up the day's Buddhist demonstrations. M. Ottavj's life could probably be measured by the number of broken bottles and empty tear-gas canisters he had seen in the streets of Saigon.

*

A series of incidents occurred partly in M. Ottavj's hotel about which I wrote for my newspaper that concerned the character of a South Vietnamese soldier in the midst of the war, and that were finally bundled together and published under the common title *Vien Goes to War*. Captain Vien's escapades sum up quite neatly all that I felt about the bravery or otherwise of the soldiers of the South Vietnamese Army – not, I hasten to add, most of its senior officers – which since the war ended have been treated with a largely unjustified contempt. The average soldier of South Vietnam was badly led by senior officers who were often corrupt, cowardly and inefficient. But that didn't mean that the average Vietnamese in uniform was likewise corrupt, cowardly and inefficient. That perhaps needs saying again, because it has something important to say about Vietnam in general, about both Hanoi and Ho Chi Minh City, in this time of reunification and common nationhood.

Accordingly I repeat the entire short saga of Captain Vien, who was, in some sort, a typical soldier of the South, and one, incidentally, of whom I have had no news whatsoever since 1974.

VIEN GOES TO WAR

A Vietnamese friend called Vien stopped me the other day in a Saigon street. I had not seen him for some time. We had first met when I went, six years ago, to a Saigon pagoda to see if I could interview the leading monk there, Thich Tri Quang, the turbulent, so-called neutralist priest who was giving the Americans a lot of trouble – he wanted to get rid of them and negotiate peace with the Communist North. Vien had been sitting at the entrance to the pagoda as I waited. A skinny young fellow, his English was bad, but he was friendly in the inevitable Vietnamese way. He invited me to meet his family. They lived in a tiny house crowded with relatives near Cholon, the predominantly Chinese quarter of the city. Vien himself was at school – at least in theory. His father was a very minor civil servant. An elder brother was in the United States, learning to be a jet pilot.

Now here was Vien again, grinning, explaining that now he was an Army captain, married for two years. Next day he came to see me at my small hotel. He carried his tiny daughter, who clutched a large red balloon. 'I killed two Vietcong last night,' he said.

'Killed? In Saigon?'

'Yes. I was patrolling the streets with my security platoon at 3 a.m. and there they were.' The curfew started at 1 a.m. 'When I saw these two men in soldiers' uniform on a motor scooter, I shouted to them to stop. But they didn't stop, so I opened fire and we ran up the road. They fired back and my major was grazed on the wrist. But we killed them.'

In the middle of town? Or on the edge of Saigon?

'No, in So-and-So Street – not very far from this hotel,' Vien grinned. 'My major say I very good captain, okay.'

His daughter struggled and let go of the balloon. It floated up to the ceiling, far out of reach. We looked at the baby, worried she would begin to howl, but she didn't.

I was packing to leave Saigon for the Delta, and Vien saw a tie I had put out. 'Number one. I take that.'

We went down to the street and he threw a leg over the saddle of his scooter, one arm round the baby. 'Petrol *very* expensive now,' he said, smiling in a way he intended to be disarming. So I gave him 500 piastres, not much. 'I'll pay you back,' he called, driving off.

A few days later I had returned and he came to see me again, this time without the baby. He kicked off his boots and lay down on my bed without asking. One of the two Vietcong men he'd stopped and fired on had not died – had only been mildly wounded, in fact. 'I've spent all day today interrogating him,' said Vien, yawning and stretching. 'Very tiring.'

Well, what had he confessed?

'He confessed he joined the Vietcong when he was twelve. He's twenty-five now. He comes from the north of South Vietnam, and went with his family to North Vietnam some years ago. He's been in a military officers' school up there. Earlier this year he came down south through the Ho Chi Minh trail, through Laos and Cambodia.'

Did he say all this quite freely?

'Well,' Vien grinned, 'not quite freely at first.'

'What did you do – pull out his fingernails?'

'Oh, no. We attached his fingers and feet to the electric current and switched it on now and again. Sometimes we poured water down his throat.'

'I see. And what else did he say?'

'He's been living in the An Quang pagoda in Saigon. You know the monks are very loving people. Anyone can go and live there – me, even you,' Vien smiled. 'No need to have proper identity cards. He told the monks he is from Hué and they accepted that. And, of course, he was a soldier because he appeared in uniform. Very clever, the VC.'

Did he admit to any specific objective?

'He had orders to blow up two bridges in Saigon. He carried a Chinese pistol and some plastic – enough to blow up a bridge or two.'

I wondered if his plan was part of a general attack on Saigon.

'That's what I must make him tell me tomorrow morning,' said Vien. 'I told him I'd be back tomorrow morning and that he'd get a bad time if he didn't tell me.' Vien left then, but soon popped back. 'You know what? My general has sent a message he wants to see me on Monday.'

'What for?' I asked. 'To make you a major?'

'No, no, I am only just a captain. No, but I think he is very pleased with me.' Vien's excitement was shining into the room. 'I think he'll give me money. Oh, I don't know how much. But he must be pleased that I caught those VC.'

'That's good for you,' I said.

'Yes, thank you,' grinned Vien. 'Oh, by the way, could you lend me another 500 piastres? I'll pay you back on Monday. Sorry, but I spend money on girls too much.'

His grin didn't look sorry at all, and of course he is married, but I gave it to him. And he threw out a dinner invitation from his mother. Of course I accepted.

Not long ago, I remembered, Vien had been visibly upset when, as he left a café, a dog was run over by a scooter in front of us and badly mangled. His parents' little, overcrowded, mosquito-ridden house was destroyed by American bombing during the 1968 Tet offensive, when the Vietcong came into his part of Saigon. They got compensation for that – perhaps because his brother is a pilot and trained in America. Vien used to like to visit the zoo. He was rather short-sighted, on the shy side and gentle.

Now he's a captain, goes after Vietcong for a living, and the money goes on girls. At least he adores his baby girl and buys her a balloon every day.

Two weeks ago Vien was sent for by his major and told to go to the extreme northern city of Quang Tri, which was captured by North Vietnamese troops this week. 'Pick up some North Vietnamese prisoners who have decided to defect and come back,' said the major.

Excited, Vien came round to my hotel. He sat on my bed and screwed up his face in mock tragedy. 'I must go to Quang Tri,' he wailed, rocking miserably back and forth. 'Many, many VC there. Maybe I die.'

'Maybe you get a medal,' I said.

'No want a medal,' wailed Vien. 'Want to stay in Saigon.'

'Maybe they make you a major,' I said.

'No want to be a major. Want to be captain – even lieutenant – and stay in Saigon.'

He seized my arm. 'When I tell my mother and father I go to Quang Tri they cry very, very much.' He ran his fingers down his cheeks indicating tears. Even so, he was half grinning. 'I know – maybe I give my major some money not to go to Quang Tri. But I haven't enough money. Could you . . . ?'

'No,' I said.

Vien shook his head. He stood up, polished his stars of rank before my wall mirror and walked over to put his hands on my shoulders. 'I will not say goodbye,' he said in mildly tragic tones. 'That's bad luck. So – see you soon.' He made a consciously slow, sad exit, backwards.

Three days later he came again to see me, bounding in, full of life and pride. 'It was nothing,' he said happily. 'Now I can go to Quang Tri any time and not be afraid.' It seemed he had brought back a North Vietnamese colonel and a major among other soldiers of Hanoi's Army who had been captured and then defected.

'Do you think the North Vietnamese will come all the way down to Saigon?' I asked him.

'No, no, no . . . impossible. We cannot have North Vietnamese in here. No good. No good,' said Vien indignantly.

'But you are North Vietnamese.' His family, I knew, was originally from the North.

'Yes,' Vien grinned, 'but I am good North Vietnamese. I believe about Buddha. Hanoi is like you, not believing.'

A week later, back he came to my hotel. 'I'm off to An Loc.' He looked unhappy. 'No want to go,' he said.

An Loc is about 60 miles northwest of Saigon and has been the scene of a furious battle involving tanks and infantry for three weeks. I thought this sounded more dangerous than his mission to Quang Tri. I had been ambushed on the road to An Loc the same week. But I didn't say so to Vien.

'I am going to collect more prisoners. You think I will die?'

'Of course not,' I said.

A few days later he was back. He fell, beaming, into the room like a puppy with a bone. He might have taken the whole North Vietnamese Army on single-handed and routed it.

'Phew! You know An Loc full of V C,' he said. 'When we came down over An Loc in our American helicopter I saw all those soldiers sitting on tanks in the streets. Some were drinking soft drinks outside shops, and I think they must be our men. But my major says no, those are all North Vietnamese. I am so shocked and so scared, I fall out of our helicopter on my head. Very painful.' Vien laughed and rubbed a large lump on his forehead . . . 'Sorry, must go,' he said soon. 'I must go to see prisoners – I brought back thirteen. Then I go to hospital to see my brother.' Vien's brother was shot down recently and lost his left hand – something Vien accepts quite unsentimentally.

I think Vien is typical of many South Vietnamese trapped in this appalling impasse. He is not urging an end to the war at any price, though he very much wants peace. He does want the moderate General 'Big' Minh to be President, and thinks the Americans' friend, General Thieu, too dictatorial and too corrupt. But for now he is plodding on with his military life, hoping to be a major, periodically scared stiff and periodically proud.

Not all South Vietnamese soldiers – we all know this by now – are the best in the world, and after all these grinding years of war, why should they be? Some run away and some do not; but, significantly, on the whole they do not desert. There has been panic here and there in the face of oncoming North Vietnamese tanks these last weeks, but no units have gone over to the North

Vietnamese, although opportunity was certainly knocking. I believe this is important – and it should always be remembered, whoever wins this war. It means the Communists are not winning the hearts and minds of the South Vietnamese despite the corruption and incompetence in Saigon.

There is a striking calmness about many Vietnamese soldiers in the field – the calm of Buddhist fatalism, perhaps. Not long ago, I was crouching in an inadequate trench with North Vietnamese mortar bombs dropping here and there. I looked up to see a small, round, laughing face peering down at me, a face almost extinguished by a huge helmet: a Vietnamese soldier. Between his teeth he gripped a small, gold-coloured Buddha that was attached to a thin chain round his neck. He was far more exposed than I was, but he was calmly motioning with his hand for me to take care and get down further; he might have been my affectionate friend. Sometimes when I think of the South Vietnamese Army I think of that brave laughing face and people like Vien.

So the heroes were not all on one side; any more than all the villains were soldiers.

A passage in the North Vietnamese veteran Bao Ninh's novel, *The Sorrow of War*, recently revealed to me something of the malice and contempt that controlled the rulers of Vietnam after the victory of 1975; the venom which, apart from anything else, created an exodus of some of the best brains in the country which could, and should, have been recruited in the Battle for the Economy.

Bao Ninh remembers the 'Unification' troop train that took the soldiers back to the north after the fall of Saigon.

At every station the loudspeakers blared, blasting the ears of the wounded, the sick, the blind, the mutilated, the white-eyed, grey-lipped malarial troops. Into their ears poured an endless stream of the most ironic of teachings, urging them to ignore the spirit of reconciliation, to beware of the 'bullets' coated with sugar, to ignore the warmth and passions among the remnants of the fallen, luxurious society of the South. *And especially to guard against the idea of the South having fought valiantly or been meritorious in any way* [the italics are mine].

But we 'meritorious' and 'victorious' soldiers knew how to defend ourselves against this barrage of nonsense. We made fun of the loudspeakers' admonishment, turning their speeches into jokes, ridiculing them.

Genuine reunification is here at last. But no wonder it took so long coming. No wonder Mme Bong's family endured seven years in hard labour camps and are now in permanent exile. No wonder Mr Thai said to me then, 'Everyone in the country is an informer. We have to be very careful.' No wonder he repeated, '*Everyone*, Mr Young.'

While I was at the Royal, I had grown used to the sudden drunken incursions into Jean Ottavj's bar of bands of American redneck civilians. These pests – I may have grown used to them but I still regarded them as pests – worked for a construction company based somewhere in one of the southernmost states of the United States, perhaps Texas. They were almost without exception obese and obscene; their enormous stomachs swollen by too much beer overflowed belts that barely managed to hold up their trousers. They were usually drunk at any time in the evening after seven o'clock; and they were disorderly bullies, too, and flagrant womanizers. I was convinced that these grotesque men – overpaid and under no one's control (the American Military Police seemed to ignore them) – made more enemies for America, turning more Vietnamese into sympathizers of the Viet Cong than even the GIs with their habit of torching innocent hamlets.

One day early in the year – it was almost Tet holiday time – I met a genuine South Vietnamese hero. A young lieutenant in the South Vietnamese Army, he had been taken prisoner by the Viet Cong somewhere in the Delta, near Ben Tré perhaps, and held there by them for several days until he managed to escape in a particularly courageous manner. On his arrival in Saigon, newly at liberty, he had been paraded at a news conference, and incidentally was awarded an obviously well-deserved medal by the South Vietnamese Army. After the press conference I happened to meet him, and I invited him and his brand-new wife (he had introduced a girl of extreme beauty) to dinner one night during the forthcoming holiday weekend. I wanted to give them a treat.

We met, as planned; he, as handsome as a film star, in a smart, freshly pressed uniform and his new medal-ribbon on his chest; she in a beautiful *ao dai*, which made her with her long black hair flowing down her back and her lovely oval face even more beautiful than she had appeared before. They stood waiting for me outside M. Ottavj's hotel door looking as fine and good-looking a couple as you could possibly imagine, and because I couldn't think of anywhere that would make the evening quite so special for both of them, I had booked a table at the roof-top restaurant of the Caravelle. I gave them dinner and a goodish wine and later in the street once more, we walked a short block to Nguyen Hué Street and strolled in the cool of a superb moonlit evening among the stalls set up there by flower sellers – I believe I bought the officer's smiling wife a bouquet of gladioli wrapped in cellophane. The war, for once, seemed far away.

After that, laughing and cheerful, we wandered back towards the corner of Nguyen Thiep Street where they would say goodnight to me, having called it a day. But things did not turn out as I had hoped to make a happy evening perfect. As we waited on the kerb, a jeepload of those American construction workers swept round the corner and deliberately pulled up alongside us.

In the jeep's passenger seat was a more than usually obese character in cowboy boots with the remains of a thick cigar between his lips. Removing the cigar-stub from obscenely thick lips (incidentally revealing that two of his front teeth were missing) he leaned towards the beautiful girl in her *ao dai* and shouted at her in the coarsest way possible, 'You wanna fuck', while the jeepload of his friends guffawed with glee. The girl, I should have explained, did not understand one word of English, so she stood there smiling prettily, presumably believing that the American had paid her a compliment. But her husband – the handsome medal winner – certainly understood. Furious, he grabbed his wife's hand, tore her away from all of us, and raced with her up the street. I never saw either of them again.

Chapter 11

All that I have written above about the war tries to explain why young Vietnamese today do not like talking about the war, and do not even try to imagine it. That is why they are so lovable, and why they so much love life as they have it now.

It is sometimes hot in Saigon. Back at the Givral Coffee House, old men are playing cards and draughts on a shaded part of the pavement. A young man passes, balancing a tray of cakes on his head. A beggar hurries, as best he can on one leg, after two middle-aged Americans in shorts and baseball caps who cross the street, dangerously, through thick traffic. The Americans try in vain to shake him off; it is embarrassing to thrust away a sweating man with one leg.

A stout, middle-aged Vietnamese woman selling postcards on a tray, shouts at me, 'Hey, long time no see!' It certainly is a long time – about ten years, I should think. But she doesn't pursue me; it is a friendly shout, like the shouts of waiters in the Givral who apologize when the electricity is cut off and the temperature rises sharply. 'It is not your fault,' I tell them, and they smile and nod and begin to open windows and doors to let in fresh air.

The sun is shining and the streets now *are* very hot. Wang, the newspaper seller, looks in through the window and grins and waves, his face wet with sweat. Inside, people fan themselves with the menus.

*

It will be cooler in the Delta, says my friend, Tam, from the tourist bureau, there's more breeze and more open space. And of course the water everywhere cools things down.

Tet – the Vietnamese New Year – was approaching and Tam had suggested we take a trip to the south, to the Delta. Her home is there in Can Tho, and it is a long time, of course, since I was there. I want to see – I tell her – the place near Chau Doc, where Minh's son Bao, then nine years old, and Ho Trang's second son Ly, then about eighteen, escaped from Vietnam into Cambodia on their way to the United States. The place is called Hông Ngu; it is very near the Cambodian border on the Mekong River.

So Tam and I set out on the road from Saigon to the Delta; the same road that Ly and little Bao had taken in January 1988, when they left Saigon at four o'clock one morning by bus. They, too, had left via Cholon, as we did. The big difference was that Tam and I were secure in a car driven by Mr Ky, Tam's driver, and Ly and Bao had been in a group of seven fearful refugees, all strangers to them and to each other.

'We had water and two tins of condensed milk,' Ly had told me as we sat calmly talking about it much later in a hotel room in New York City. 'And we had a little money, $5 each, so we could buy food on the road.'

Ly also told me that Mr Long, from the Ho Chi Minh City press office, whom I had thought was so generous the year I was there with Mr Thai for the tenth anniversary parade, had put $300 of the $400 I had given him to pass on to Minh's family, into his own pocket. So much for generosity, I thought. Well, at least it had worked in the end.

So on the road through Cholon – it seemed to go on and on and the traffic, mostly bicycles and motorbikes, was appalling – Tam and I took the path that Ly and Bao had taken years before.

I could imagine the fear they felt as the cold morning air poured in through the bus's windows and the sun slowly came up out of the sea to their left. It turned out that they had every right to be fearful. Their immediate future was dire.

The first time I saw Mme Bong on my return to Saigon in 1995 she asked after her exiled family, 'How is Viet?' (Minh's younger son and Bao's small brother, now about fifteen).

'Very well.'

'He is so naughty.'

'Very intelligent, too.'

'I know,' she said. 'Very. And is Bao as serious as ever?'

'As always.'

Then I asked her, 'When Bao left to escape to Cambodia with Ly were you afraid for him? Was *he* afraid?'

Mme Bong answered, 'I was very afraid. But Bao said, "Death is better than this life."' She paused. 'You saw them in the camp in Thailand?'

'No, the Thais would not allow me to.' She nodded, and I went on, 'Isn't Vu the spitting image of his father?' Vu's father, Van, was killed in 1967. He was Mme Bong's eldest son. For a moment she looked surprised. 'Did you meet Van?' she asked.

'I remember sitting in the upstairs window in Hué with Van and Minh and Qué watching the midnight parade of cyclo drivers, and the women who had been chewing betel, and students shouting for the resignation of Thieu and the withdrawal of the Americans.'

Mme Bong cried, 'What a memory you have! You remember everything!'

She repeated this when I mentioned the little dog she had in the house in Hué. I remembered the dog very well; Mimi was her name. One day she snatched the chicken off the dining table.

After a bit, Mme Bong said, 'I like Ly very much.'

'So do I,' I said. Ly was in Virginia now, trying to be a doctor.

After another pause she said with great earnestness, 'Please help Minh if you can.'

'Of course I will,' I said. 'But it is difficult. You know how obstinate Minh is.'

'Oh, yes,' she said and smiled.

'Whenever I offer him money he refuses it very forcefully. I did help Ho Trang to buy his house,' I went on. 'Minh has rented his own now, as I expect you know. But it isn't easy to help him.'

Mme Bong said, 'Please try. You were wonderful with Ho Trang. But Minh is so poor and he does work so hard. Sixteen hours a day.'

To comfort her, I said, 'Don't worry. I shall keep an eye on him. And Bao and Viet, too.'

She told Vu in French to take good care of me and not to drive too fast on the way back to my hotel. Vu speaks no French at all and not much English. But I suppose he got the gist of what she said because he regularly pointed proudly at the speedometer on the way back. It said twenty-five kilometres an hour for most of the way. It took us quite a time to reach the Asian Hotel.

The morning Ky drove me to see the Cu Chi tunnels and the Cao Dai city of Tay Ninh, the lobby of the Asian Hotel was bustling with middle-aged men and women from Europe and America in unwise shorts, which they increasingly insist on wearing and which display their worst physical attributes: huge buttocks and stomachs predominating.

Thus before we had even set out a serious problem posed itself. Why – the question went – do relatively affluent tourists of a certain age demean themselves by leaving their hotels in wholly inadequate clothing? Vietnamese, among the poorest people in the world and with ridiculously small salaries, manage to dress in a dignified way, the humblest Vietnamese wouldn't dream of appearing in public in tight shorts that would expose huge buttocks and skinny or over-plump legs, still less would they go into the street in anything less than long-sleeved shirts (perhaps, it is true, with the sleeves rolled up to their elbows) and long trousers.

It's a question of dignity, I suppose. Vietnamese cling proudly to their dignity. It's one thing they have left. Americans, and increasingly Europeans, seem determined, on the other hand, to degrade themselves to the utmost. It is a strange and worrying phenomenon. If Ho Chi Minh was alive would he allow all these foreigners, obviously lacking in self-respect, to set such a bad example to his people? It is probably just as well he is not around to answer that question.

At any rate, these chubby tourists could hardly fit into the narrow tunnels of Cu Chi. Neither could I for that matter. We drove about thirty kilometres out of Saigon to get to them; thirty kilometres of low shops on both sides of the road – Honda repair shops, shops where logs of wood or bamboo were being sawn up and turned into tables and chairs, and the occasional barber's shop with men lying back in ramshackle chairs being shaved by other men in shirt-sleeves. Later on we turned off the main road and passed through small hamlets with an occasional Cao Dai temple with its single ever-open eye watching us over the gate. Was it to counter the influence of the eye that Ky, the driver, smartly turned up his cassette player and deluged us with the deafening sound of old pop songs like 'Itsy-bitsy, teeny-weeny yellow polka-dot bikini' and 'I saw Mommy kissing Santa Claus' until I begged him to switch it off again? Soon we were bowling along through the flat, well-watered rice fields, water buffaloes wallowing in mud and waves of white egrets that flew low over the paddy and half-hidden roofs of small houses, ponds full of ducks, and women in conical hats and black pyjamas up to their calves in water.

It was somewhere near Cu Chi where the road dipped and plunged into clumps of reeds, I remember, that the convoy of trucks and ammunition wagons I was riding in, towards Tay Ninh which the North Vietnamese Army was attacking from Cambodia, was ambushed. Mortar bombs started dropping around us; some of them much too close for comfort. The convoy pulled up with a shudder and we all bailed out of our trucks.

I crawled away and came to rest on the road's verge under the large protective belly of a more than usually big military vehicle. I could just see a colleague and friend, Donald Wise of the *Daily Express*, signalling mysteriously but urgently to me not far away, but too far for me to hear what he was shouting. Feeling it was important to know what he was trying to convey, I jumped up and dropped down beside him.

'What the hell are you trying to say?' I yelled at him.

'Just look at that big truck you were hiding under, you bloody fool,' he replied, pointing to it.

I looked to where he was pointing and as clear as daylight saw writing on the truck's big belly in large white letters: 'Danger. Flammable. Fuel'. It would only need one mortar bomb to turn it – and me – into a blazing inferno.

How was I to know that the next time I passed this way it would be more than twenty years later and it would not be an ambush by mortar bombs that would put the fear of God into me, but the 'Itsy-bitsy, teeny-weeny, yellow polka-dot bikini'?

The tunnels of Cu Chi went down to four levels beneath the ground with dining-rooms for the Viet Cong soldiers, kitchens with air vents to take the cooking smoke up to the outer air, lecture rooms and briefing rooms, and walls which had been widened postwar to allow tourists to pass through them without getting stuck, brought on, in me at least, so acute an attack of claustrophobia that I couldn't face the crawl I would have to make to get from one part of the tunnel system to another.

I was obliged to confess shamefully to Ky (he took it inscrutably well) that sheer funk would not permit me to descend even to the first level down. I imagined the roof caving in on me and myself stuck down there for ever.

As a result, my view of the Cu Chi tunnels was limited to contemplating with awe the bravery of American soldiers in the war who had, I had read, plunged down the tunnels after the Viet Cong with the agility of ferrets after rabbits, incidentally risking (and often incurring) severe wounds to their feet from the spikes that the enemy had embedded at suitable spots.

On the road to Tay Ninh, by now denuded of the watchtowers that used to stretch along the roadside like skeletal sentries in the time of the French war, the signs of the Cao Daists multiplied. Here and there in the villages and hamlets on the way the pale blue, yellow and pink plasterboard Cao Dai churches poked gaily through the rows of poor stalls and shops like marzipan-covered wedding cakes, and over their gates the ever-open eye of God regarded us balefully. Small boys sat on the backs of buffaloes that wallowed in the water and mud of paddy fields on either side of the road, while the tourist buses and cars whizzed past towards the sacred mountain which loomed in the distance like, as Greene said, a green bowler hat.

I had intended to stay the night in Tay Ninh, see the Cao Dai cathedral in the morning and visit the sacred mountain that evening. But there were hotel problems in Tay Ninh.

The Hao Binh Hotel, huge and empty, was barely functional. One light in four worked in the large $20-a-night room I was offered. It was also hot; the air conditioning unit had an asthmatic cough and spat out warm air. So I moved to the Anh Dao Hotel down the road. It was slightly better, but by then it was past 6.30 p.m. At least at the Anh Dao the air conditioning worked, and so did some of the lights. I decided to eat and sleep early, and with Ky, the driver, I went to an open-air restaurant where we drank BGI beer and ate rice and soup with *nuoc mam*, the Vietnamese fish sauce. After that Ky decided he wanted to sing for an hour or so at the local karaoke bar. I went to bed, and tried to pretend I couldn't hear a neighbouring video show which was playing Chinese kick-boxing movies with the sound turned up for the benefit, the hotel receptionist told me, of a party of Vietnamese tourists from Long Xuyen. Were they very old and deaf, I wondered?

In the end I didn't go to the sacred mountain.

I did go, though, to the 'wedding cake' Cao Dai cathedral, and then took the road back to Saigon. The church (it certainly was big enough for a cathedral) stands huge and imposing, painted in gold and blue and pink; the ever-open eye staring down from the portico and the words 'Fraternity, Humanity, Love, Justice' in large letters were framed in it. Inside the building, which echoed impressively, a voice said in my ear, 'All truths are united in Cao Daism and truth is love'. I looked past the nun with a shaven head who had said this at twenty-eight pillars up which dragons were climbing, thrusting out hideously gaping mouths. The nun, slowly following me, went on to intone, 'One for every bright star in the heavens', whatever she meant by that. The trouble was she spoke without accent or intonation, as if she was drugged. This, I thought, as Graham Greene had done forty years before me in this very spot, was not the Vietnam I loved. My eyes followed the dragons disappearing into the lofty, sky-blue vaulting in the ceiling of the glittering pastel nave. This was a place of interminable ceremonies. Soon monks and nuns, seven hundred of them or so I suppose, filed into the vast nave, formed up in neat rows and began chanting in unison while a small string orchestra struck up in the gallery.

There was something of Buddhism, Christianity and Confucianism in the Cao Dai religion, a synthesis which had been the brainchild of a Vietnamese civil servant in the 1920s. That explained paintings and images of an improbable 'Saint' Victor Hugo, Confucius, and Sun Yat Sen writing on a scroll near the entrance. Swallows flitted about the towering nave of the church, while my nun droned on inexorably in my ear, 'There are seven million Cao Daists in Vietnam'; her voice was like a gramophone record. 'Shaven heads are voluntary.' To my surprise, Victor Hugo wore a cocked hat, presiding over rows of golden chairs, and the dragons and snakes intertwined on the ceiling gave the whole gaudily painted building the look of a marzipan-coated cake and the feeling of a Walt Disney production.

Chapter 12

Even before I met Vu outside my Saigon hotel, I had noticed in Hanoi the miraculous change that had taken place since 1965, leave alone since 1985. On a second visit, flying from Bangkok into Tan San Nhat airport at Ho Chi Minh City, the new (optional) name for Saigon, the Thai Airbus raised one great wing like the sail of a windmill and dived down through light cloud. In 1965 this had always been the nasty moment – the moment of truth, some journalists had joked. One expected a terrific jolt and a sickening plunge as a missile struck the plane before it twisted its way down to earth and oblivion.

These days there is nothing to worry about; only the harmless rush of air and, directly below, neat red roofs lining the waterways that surround the city. The Saigon River meanders beneath us and all is peaceful. I saw the bridge that was gallantly defended in vain by South Vietnamese paratroopers against the advancing Northerners in the last bloody days of the city's resistance in April 1975. It was a relief to know that smoke billowing up behind a clump of palm trees could not possibly have been caused by a mortar bomb or a flame-thrower, that it was harmless, only a bonfire.

There were no golden temples either as there would have been in Thailand, where the plane had come from. Just a few ramshackle fortified posts left over from the war and a few unmanned anti-aircraft guns pointing skywards. Then we were down and taxiing through lines of Airbuses and Boeings of Vietnam Airlines. It had been called Air

Vietnam in 1965 and the planes then were DC-4s and DC-6s, and American fighters had crouched in the hump-backed bomb- and rocket-proof shelters that we rolled past after we had left behind the new passenger jets – the Thai and Cathay Pacific 747s – that have replaced the wartime Caribous, the C-124s and the C-130 transports.

That first day back was like a homecoming. Viet and Tam, my two new friends from the tourist bureau in Saigon, met me at the airport and drove me to my hotel, a new one to me in what had been rue Catinat, then Tu Do Street, and was now Dong Khoi Street.

The Asian was a new hotel but the street itself was very familiar. The art gallery two doors down the street I seemed to remember had been a bar in which years before I had exchanged greetings with my colleague, the Visnews photographer Neal Davis, who was sitting there with a girl a few years before he was killed, of all places, in Bangkok during a military coup. There were other changes, too. The 'Continental shelf', the open terrace of the Continental Hotel, had been glassed-in and has become an Italian restaurant, and opposite it the Caravelle was having an extension tacked on to it by, I think, a Japanese company.

On the corner opposite the Continental Hotel still stood my favourite coffee house, the Givral, which I was to use during the next year as much as I always had in wartime.

The Givral, it is true, had become a haven for beggars – or rather the pavement on the corner outside had. I soon enlisted an ally to ward them off. Young Wang is a small but very tough newspaper seller; a sort of Vietnamese Artful Dodger. He is usually on patrol outside the Givral with his stack of newspapers, and his friend who wears a dirty baseball cap. I make a habit of buying an *International Herald Tribune* from Wang every afternoon and tipping him moderately once or twice a week. Wang enlists his tiny, but eminently tough and streetwise friends to shield me – when they remember to – from the more aggressive beggars: scrawny mothers with drugged and filthy babies in their arms, the youngish man with stumps for hands and malformed feet who seldom leaves me alone, shouting at me, 'Hey, you!' waving his stumps, graphically explaining 'an American bomb blew up – B O O M!' I usually give him a couple of dollars, although I realize he is far too young to have been in the war. I suppose he might more recently have found an unexploded bomb. In any case his mutilations are horrific. When Wang sees this man is overdoing things, he and his chums move in to shield me. They see my greying hair and call me 'Pappa', which I find I don't mind at all. From a friend of Wang's, for $2, I bought a Zippo cigarette lighter, an exact imitation of the lighters the GIs used to carry. This one had an inscription that said, 'Hué 1968', and another that said, 'If I had a farm in Vietnam and a home in hell, I'd sell my farm and go home' – a good example of cynical GI wit.

Moving on down Dong Khoi Street – Dong Khoi means 'Revolution', I am told by friendly Vietnamese – past the huge Philips sign, past the old Air France office and the new Cathay Pacific office, towards the Majestic Hotel and the Saigon River, the wartime past catches up with one. In the French time, landing-craft tied up in the river outside that grand hotel (less grand than now) for repairs, Greene said, as noisy as 'road drills in a London summer'.

'Will independence come too late?' Greene had wondered, as the lift carried him to the top floor where ten years later I and Donald Wise listened to a Vietnamese singer whose name – or so Donald swore – was Ngoc My. 'Has control of the Viet Minh movement passed irrevocably into the hands of the communists? Has Ho Chi Minh been converted to the solution by violence which he so long opposed, or is he a virtual prisoner in communist hands?' Greene could find nothing but uniform pessimism in his own inadequate answers to these silent questions. A decade later, we couldn't do much better.

There had been a danger, people believed in 1954, that if no agreement was reached between the French and the Vietnamese on independence, weariness and division might suggest quack remedies. The 'pipedream of substituting American for French Union troops', for example, which might lead to a massive defeat, grew from a pipedream, as we all know, into a reality which abandoned many non-communist Vietnamese nationalists to the mercy of their enemies.

Many years later we felt an equal depression.

Now, however, I felt, on the contrary, a great elation because despite everything that had happened, the sound of bombs had stopped, no flares trickled down the night sky, nobody was being killed, even the flood of refugees out of Vietnam had come to an end. And thinking this at the door of the newly painted and tarted-up Majestic, I suddenly saw alongside the jetty the *My Canh* floating restaurant.

The *My Canh*!

When I saw that tragic relic, I stood quite still, unable to move, paralysed with the remembered image of that poor blood-soaked wreck after it had been struck by the Viet Cong claymore mine that exploded one evening among the diners. That was in 1965, when I hadn't been in Vietnam long. As the survivors tottered down the gangplank, I recalled now, escaping in a daze the horror of limbless civilians and eviscerated children, a second claymore mine, carefully aimed in advance at the survivors, went off as they tried to get ashore. It cut them down with solid chunks of metal as they came down the gangway.

I forget how many died in the wreckage of the *My Canh*. Now there was the *My Canh*, under my eyes, restored to life. At least I suppose it was the same vessel; now I wonder if it could have been a substitute.

On my second visit, I marched straight into the Majestic's grand entrance and under its chandeliers up to the reception desk. In no time at all I had booked myself into a room facing the river and told the receptionist that I would be back to occupy it in two days' time. I left two days blank because I wanted time to think; and time, too, to explore more of this part of the city where so much had occurred that had so influenced my life.

So in two days I was back at the Majestic. I had remembered the

Bank of India – the two small shops run by Indian merchants where in American times we changed our piastres into Black Market dollars (or vice versa) – the difference in the exchange was quite considerable then, although there is no Black Market today.

I found notes I had made in 1985 – that black Stalinist period. Even then though I had scribbled that Ho Chi Minh City was 'like a bottle of champagne – or a prolonged charge of electricity. <u>Of course</u> [I had underlined these two words] these loving, adorable people are my favourites in the world.' Even then, urchins selling cakes, deliberately bumped into me, grinned, gasped 'ooh' at my height, and melted away; and four sailors in the Rex beer parlour called 'Come over', told me their names (Xa, Duong, Ut and Chinh) and that they had a small boat in the river. They bought me beer and smiled and joked as if there had been no war, no trouble of any kind.

It was like that now – in 1995; exactly like that, only much, much better.

I leaned on the balustrade of my room at the Majestic and looked down at the towering lights of the ocean-going ships in the harbour and the neon of the numerous signs advertising Japanese and American imported goods – Honda, Sony TV, Coca-Cola, Hewlett Packard. In the street immediately below me, Vietnamese seethed in a great laughing human flood: young men in jeans, white shirts, the girls in jeans and blouses and now and again in round, Dresden-shepherdess straw hats decorated with flowers. Once silk-trousered girls had moved gracefully down this street in the hard noon's glare. Now older men and women perched on the pillions of their children's motorbikes or bicycles, grasping them round the waist. I watched them laughing and shouting, heading across the short foot bridges that linked the shore and the floating bars and restaurants (the *My Canh* was far from being the only one).

I concentrated on a group of four young men and girls, saw them

shouting with glee, pretending to push each other into the river under
the trees and the bright lights on the public footpath that links the
bank. They seemed to typify the new Vietnamese as well as the young,
carefree Vietnamese I seemed to have left behind thirty years before.
'Age drops suddenly like the sun,' somebody has truly said. 'Vietnamese
are boys – and then they are old men.'

I thought of all those years of war that had gone by. No one, of all
those beneath me, who was under (say) thirty-five years old, could
remember the fighting. Except the maimed, of course. Today the average
Vietnamese doesn't want to so much as *think* of war: he wants a Honda
and a fistful of dollars.

Well, that wasn't so bad. Better than what had gone before, at least.

I yawned and stretched. I suddenly felt tired. I would have one whisky
and turn in. I had to meet Tam next morning; she would take me for
a trip up the river which I knew so well by sight but on which I had
never been.

Tam was there punctually as usual, and we walked to the river bank
where she knew a reliable boatman with a covered launch.

We swung out into midstream and started upriver, past floating
restaurants parked on both banks and the dignified Riverside Hotel
with a date on it: 1864, which means it was built in the last years of
the American Civil War, and the grand towering modern outline of the
Floating Hotel. Then, past two dry docks, the banks frayed out into
poverty and the countryside. Houses on stilts lined the river and over
tiny inlets down which, in times past, guerrillas might have lurked,
there were duckboard bridges, looking impossibly frail and narrow,
spanning waterways among palm trees and tall grass that half hid an
occasional thatched roof. Wooden barges thrust down the river which
was a muddy brown here and about as wide as the Thames at Chelsea.
The barges were hull-down, loaded with sand, and on their bows had
been painted two eyes which seemed to frown at all they saw.

At about halfway point, Tam announced that we were approaching Binh Quoi tourist village, an attractively laid-out collection of shady bamboo cafés and restaurants on the river. Here several Vietnamese looked up from their coffees and condensed milk to watch us disembark from the rocking boat. ('Careful, Poppa,' said the boatman, taking my arm. I smiled. I noticed he had 'Scoundrel' stencilled on his T-shirt, and hoped it was not an accurate trade description.)

With Tam I order a beer, and the waiter examined the glass to see if it was clean: a good sign, particularly as the beer is a 333 – numbers which will always be associated in my mind with Vietnam, because it was such a popular drink during the war.

I find myself telling Tam how the Thai driver who took me from Bangkok airport to my hotel asked me, 'Have you been many times to Vietnam?'

'Yes. Many times.'

'Is it a nice place?'

'Very nice. Very poor.'

Now I turn to Tam and add: 'It is very poor. I know that. Well, I think I like poor places if they're like this.'

Tam said seriously: 'Yes. I really think you do.'

I gazed happily at the sun-baked palms and the bamboo roofs of the tourist village's cafés, and at the muddy water of the Saigon River, and said to her, with feeling, 'Yes, you know,' I said, 'I really do.'

There was a container port further upriver and a ship undergoing repairs in one of them, the *Fair Fortune* from Panama. Later, women were paddling in sampans under a bridge which may have been the one leading from Saigon to Bien Hoa, and which had been in 1975 the scene of a furious fire-fight when the South Vietnamese paratroopers tried in vain to stem the North Vietnamese advance into the city.

I had visited the young paras in their training camp in Saigon in 1974. Swinging down on practice ropes, they were strong, smart-looking fellows in camouflaged uniforms, and one had asked me (thinking I was an American, I suppose), 'You have abandoned us. Please tell us why, sir.' I had nothing to tell him. Perhaps he died on that bridge we were passing under now.

In 1995 I left the Majestic, where in 1985 I had met that official of the People's Committee who had lectured us on re-education camps and political prisoners, and crossed the road to the bank of the Saigon River. Tam was waiting for me there, and we boarded a similar boat to the one that had already taken us upstream. We would sail downstream today. The boat headed for mid-river and once there began to move towards the sea, or rather to follow the incredible zigzags of the river which eventually – somehow – flowed into the sea.

On its left bank nearest the city, a number of ships were loading or offloading, their derricks swinging back and forth in a frenzy of activity. Ships from Singapore, China, Cyprus, Vietnam itself, and a number of rusty hulks which could have come from anywhere. On the other side a line of ramshackle houses on stilts teetered on the edge of the water, some, unlikely as it seemed, marked 'Coffee house' and one, most unusually, 'Karaoke'. Lower down the houses ran out into fields where cattle grazed. Here, too, on the water were the same wooden barges that I had seen plodding up the river on our way up it: huge barges loaded hull down, with painted angry black eyes on their bows; their crews sheltering under an awning, sometimes playing cards there.

Ferries, too, passed us carrying waving passengers, heading from the port of Saigon and then to Vung Tau, the beach resort that was an hour away from Saigon by car. Ferry in these peaceful days is becoming the most favoured way to reach it.

Strange, I thought, how travelling by boat down this river was so much feared in the past. It was difficult not to imagine the sight and sounds of war: the fearful explosion of rockets from American helicopters, the columns of smoke billowing up, and the drumming of gunfire in the air. The whole of the area opposite Saigon where the cattle grazed had been Viet Cong territory.

I suppose one thing that made me realize that there had truly been a complete change of attitude in Saigon was my meeting with the General Manager of the Asian Hotel where I was staying. Mr Nguyen Vien Hai had been a tour guide and had then risen to a senior position in the state tourist agency, Vietnamtourism. I realized he was an honest man when he admitted to me that 'Yes, 1985 was a very hard time', and told me that his favourite book had been *The Quiet American*, a remark he made when he saw that by chance I was carrying that novel when I went to see him. 'Ah, yes, Mr Young. It was my favourite when I was in school.'

The shops in Dong Khoi Street are busy again. Every other shop seems to be selling lacquerware, silver and porcelain; antique signs follow the street to the river. There are also men selling dark glasses from trays, books of stamps and postcards. And money changers' shops (as I have said, there is no Black Market here now) sell cameras, videos and pocket calculators of all sizes.

The construction of huge, expensive buildings is going on everywhere, too. The towering silhouettes of new office blocks and grand hotels soar over central Saigon, changing the look of the city. In between them wriggles the multi-headed snake-army of Honda motorbikes, cyclos and old push-bicycles, and how they avoid appalling crashes at all the intersections with few traffic lights and policemen I cannot for the life of me tell. Accidents do happen, I am told, and a good many people bear scars to prove it, but I've never seen one. Some people even wear anti-pollution masks; what would they wear in Bangkok, where the pollution is so thick you could cut it with a knife. In Saigon there is no *visible* pollution at all.

*

In 1972 – how the years passed! – Jean Ottavj celebrated his seventieth birthday. I remember him complaining to me about the poor quality of the opium in those wartime days. His friend, Mr Yeong, the skeletal opium-parlour owner we had been to together once or twice, was dead by this time. But Ottavj, who seemed about to live for ever, always said that he himself was a moderate smoker. He ate well and drank, he said, moderate quantities of red wine with ice in it.

When I told him I had asked the British and French ambassadors to the special birthday dinner for him at the Royal, he said: '*Oh, nous sommes dans la stratosphère!*' He insisted on soup as a 'protocol dish', but I said, no, just *couscous*. Nevertheless he sneaked in *oeufs en gelée*. He also whipped up a very sweet and *very* potent 'cocktail', followed by lots of red wine and his last good bottle of *marc de bourgogne*.

His cocktail was like an atom bomb, consisting of the following ingredients: brandy and bacardi rum '*avec un peu de grenadine, m'sieu. Pour donner la couleur.*' The rim of the glasses he rubbed with lemon juice and then held them upside down to rest for a second or two in sugar. The drink tasted like a very, very sweet tequila and was as potent as Mohamed Ali's knockout punch.

Jean Ottavj had arrived in Saigon in September 1928, as a sergeant in the French army. When I say I was six months old that month, he says with a sweet smile, 'Small world, isn't it!'

The first time he ever ate frogs' legs was in an omelette in the army in Syria, he told me once. 'I could have strangled the army chef who gave me them without telling me what they were.' Then he became used to them. At that time frogs' legs and snails were hardly ever eaten in Corsica. I never saw them at the Royal. Usually M. Ottavj's restaurant at the Royal proudly featured excellent *soupe corse* (or *soupe pistou*), and *boudins noirs* (small spiced sausages). There were French air force posters on the walls and a dusty Air France flag over the bar. His TV showed old and bad French films. His waiters were mostly ancient

Vietnamese, walnut-skinned, wearing glasses; they all adored him.

At Tet one year, he said, pursing and unpursing his lips as usual: 'They are young people, all those Viet Cong. Nostradamus, the great occultist, predicted tragedy this year, did you know, *M'sieu* Young?' He began to uncork some Algerian wine. 'Fortunately I have only a few years more left to me. And I can live off a tomato and a piece of bread a day.'

Would he abandon his restaurant or his Vietnamese wife? He was indignant. 'Certainly not, *m'sieu*. After all, even the Viet Cong have to eat.'

There was nothing in the least racist about Jean Ottavj. He was never sorry for himself. Now I come to think of it, his rheumatism was appalling; he must have suffered agonies; his hands were swollen and red. One day he went for an acupuncture treatment. 'Ha!' he said to me much later. 'One man put a needle in here and in here, and in here – but instead of making me stand upright, I had to lie down for a week!' I gave him a gold disc with his initials on one side and mine on the other. It had a chain and he hung it round his neck straight away. He died wearing it in 1974. In bed; in Saigon.

Jean Ottavj could have left Vietnam and gone home to Corsica. Except for one thing. 'I have a hill in Corsica,' he said. 'And a garden. But opium is forbidden there, so *en somme, M'sieu* Young . . .' *En somme*, M. Ottavj stayed until he died in Saigon, where the opium was poor but plentiful.

Now it is 1996, and there is a wedding reception at the Continental. A long line of shining cars – the kind gangsters used to ride about in in Chicago – pulls up at the kerb outside. One car, obviously the bride's, is decorated with white and pink roses and the Chinese character meaning Good Luck.

In my hotel up the road I lie with the curtains drawn in the afternoon. I hear the put-put of the motorbikes and the very occasional shudder of a car or one of the new Mazda taxis which have meters (so that in theory one can't be ripped off by the driver).

During the war there would have been the overhead thudding of a helicopter and the rumble of gunfire from the distant paddy fields. Then suddenly the phone rings – unbelievably it is an incoming call from London, clear and untapped as far as I can tell, at least there is no suspicious sound of clicking or heavy breathing on the line. In 1985 such a call would have been unthinkable. Now my assistant, Gritta Weil, telephones me from London daily whether I'm in Saigon or Hanoi or Nha Trang or even Hué. It is as easy as calling Bangkok or Singapore. Or Paris, for that matter.

One day, after a visit to the Delta, I asked the girl receptionist at the Asian Hotel to call the number of Mme Bong's neighbour; perhaps Mme Bong herself would come to the telephone. Mme Bong came to speak to me, but she didn't seem to understand what it was I was saying. Instead Vu came round at three-thirty in the afternoon with two mangoes wrapped in a Vietnamese newspaper and a letter (written on squared paper and as always in French). I recognized the writing immediately, even after all these years. The letter said:

Dear Monsieur Young,

I will be enchanted to see you again. I am thinking you would return to Saigon later than this. This morning I realized from your call that you were back already. But I am very sorry that I could not hear you very well. I am deaf.

I hope tomorrow at noon, my grandson [Vu] will come to accompany you. Come as usual and dine with us.

I hope you are well.

I am waiting for you, dear monsieur.

A bientôt.

As usual, the letter was signed simply 'Bong'.

Perhaps that day, or perhaps later, Mme Bong reminisced about the old days in Hué.

'I took Qué's father and mother in because the father needed a job and food and she helped him. Simple as that.'

A little later, she said, 'Yes, Qué is intelligent. He always was. I paid for his schooling, as you know. He went to school with my son Minh.' She sighed. 'But Minh – no, he was not clever like Qué. Minh lacked courage. He is not brave, Minh.'

Nevertheless, she said, she loved Minh. Of course, I knew that already.

She spoke briefly to Vu, who went out of the room, returning in a short time with two photographs, framed and wrapped in paper. She said: 'I am sending these pictures to Minh. They are of my late husband.'

The photographs were copies of an old studio portrait taken in Hué – French, I suppose, of Vu's grandfather aged twenty-seven; a handsome man, obviously Vietnamese, in a suit and a bow tie. His hair was slicked back in the thirties style of the great French actor, Louis Jouvet.

He must have died shortly after this portrait was taken.

I asked Mme Bong, 'Do you own this house? Will it go to Minh's sister, Ho Trang's widow?'

'No,' said Mme Bong quietly, 'the house *may* go to Minh's sister when I die. But Ho Trang was a soldier, so the government will probably take it.'

She went on:

'Vu and his wife and his son will not be able to live here. They will have to find somewhere else.'

'Where?'

'I don't know.'

One day we talked of the old house in Hué.

'How does the house look now?' she asked.

'It's smaller.'

'Smaller. Yes, I know. The house was sold for a knockdown price to the government. I believe the new owners divided it with a wall.'

'Yes. A lady of about sixty there told me Qué's mother and father had died.'

'She told you that?'

'That's what she said, yes. But I think I knew already. Didn't Qué's father use to sit at the door rolling cheap cigarettes to sell?'

'That's right.' She smiled.

While we were chatting, I had noticed – it was difficult not to – that a deafening, aggressive crowing from a number of roosters in the passageway outside was making it hard to hear what Mme Bong was saying.

Vu, her grandson, laughed when I mentioned this.

'It's like a farmyard here,' I said to him.

Vu laughed again. 'Well, you see, these birds are for sport, not food.' It turned out that dozens of fighting cocks are confined in these backstreets under wicker cages, which let in the breeze and keep them cool while they crow at each other.

'Naturally, they indulge in crowing competitions,' Vu said. 'They are fighters.'

Mme Bong's Saigon house is not large; much smaller than the house in Hué. This one is tucked away in a back street in some western part of the city; it is difficult to find, situated as it is in a narrow alley of similar small houses. It is set back inside a tiny rectangular yard with wrought-iron railings painted blue, and consists mainly of the downstairs room we always sit and eat in. The furniture is sparse: an electric fan, one big dining table, a sofa with a plastic cover, and some utility chairs. On the walls are pictures of the family: Minh, of course; his sons, Bao and Viet; Mme Bong's two daughters (one married to Ho Trang, and the younger married to a Vietnamese in Germany, where she died recently of some sudden disease). Then there is a photograph of myself, and a portrait of Ho Trang's four sons with their mother in Virginia. That is all.

Upstairs (where I seldom cared to go) is a room of similar size where I suppose Mme Bong sleeps. I feel it is somewhere sacred to her. I know she keeps pictures of her dead daughter, her dead son Van, and her dear husband on a sort of shrine there.

I had told Mme Bong that as soon as I went to Hué I would visit the tomb of her son Van, Vu's father. He was killed in the war in 1967. And, as I have already explained, I knew and liked him.

'You took some pictures of me putting joss-sticks on his grave in Hué, didn't you?' she said.

'Yes, I did. In 1973, the year of the ceasefire.'

'Well, now the grave has been moved some way away,' Mme Bong said. 'It is still on that little hill – you know, Nui Binh. If you want to find it, ask my nephew Thieu to take you. He knows where it is.'

I wondered whether poor Van was still haunting Nui Binh, his spirit howling for his missing arm and keeping people awake. But I said nothing of this to Mme Bong.

That night I wandered down Dong Khoi Street and found myself near the place where thirty years before there had been a bar called the Miramar. The Miramar Bar was one of many popular with GIs and their Vietnamese girlfriends. One night I was sitting in there quite late watching a pretty girl on a stool talking to a tipsy GI. I began taking notes when the girl (wearing an *ao dai* and plenty of make-up) began to talk.

'It's love,' she said. 'I'm turned off completely by a guy that can't love. You know – who sits and drinks and thinks and refuses to love. Love – it's so great, right? We should all love, right?'

After a second's thought, the GI replied, 'Uh . . . well . . . yeah. It's great. But, uh, how much does that love cost around here?' I could have told him – in terms of dollars – not much. And there was the chance of a medal. Soldiers in Saigon had been awarded the Purple Heart, the medal they hand out to men wounded in action, for getting VD.

In 1985 I had noted that Saigon's shops displayed shelves of books about Lenin and paperback novels that looked horribly like Vietnamese versions of *The Love of Two Tractor Drivers* (although as tractors were not much in evidence in the countryside of Vietnam just then, a better title perhaps would have been *The Love of Two Water Buffalo Drivers*). These bookshops were dreary places, barely patronized. And the men in Hanoi, irritated by this southern lack of politico-literary seriousness, had recently begun to say so in official newspaper articles. Other articles had attacked a southern hankering for kung-fu movies, disco dancing and immodest displays of slap-and-tickle on South Vietnam's beaches.

All this was a welcome sign that humanity still breathed in Ho Chi Minh City. Another was the extraordinary and universal display of good humour and affection – not too strong a word – for foreigners like me. Everyone waved – construction workers from rooftops, girls in mollusc hats on bicycles (this was, and still is up to a point, a city of bicycles), red-faced men in cafés, peasant soldiers, rascally-looking cyclo drivers and their passengers. 'Ooh,' they cried. 'Wassname? Where you from?'

It was not that one was taken for a 'liberating' Russian comrade (the Russians were considered boorish, humourless and, above all, distressingly stingy). I announced my Englishness and the smiles widened still further. Away from the nursemaid fussiness of the official guides, I and other Westerners were enchanted Gullivers once more in a deliriously friendly Lilliput.

Chapter 13

The road to My Tho – that is the road south from Saigon; and the road to the Delta – had not changed much. Cholon had grown, it is true; it teemed with traffic (the usual motorbikes, bicycles and cyclos) and the streets seemed to go on and on until I wondered if we would ever get out of them. But at last we emerged on the more open road to Tan An, the road I remembered travelling down in a bus thirty years before with a sinister Vietnamese passenger whispering in my ear, 'What if the Viet Cong come on the bus and start shooting? They would start with you, you know.' Now I wonder if he was a Viet Cong sympathizer, deliberately trying to scare me. I was the only foreigner on board; but I was determined to stick it out and complete the journey.

At road blocks every so often, there was comfort in the sight of armed police coming on board and asking for identity cards, and at every bridge – I remember several – there was the reassuring sight of pillboxes with gun slits guarding both ends of the bridge's span which crossed one arm or another of the Mekong Delta complex.

Now over the shoulder of Mr Ky, our driver, I could see what remained of the pillboxes: derelict, black with age, surrounded with rusty barbed wire, looking as if they reeked of stale air, disuse and urine. No one had stood guard in them for at least twenty years.

Beyond My Tho came the car ferries. The Vinh Long ferry was over-cluttered with Tet traffic – buses, trucks, scooters and pick-ups queued in long lines, jostling for space. Tam and I crossed on foot, leaving the car and Mr Ky to catch up when he could. On the far side of the water, we fought our way on to a bus full of foreign backpackers, mostly Dutch. The Dutchman next to me told me he goes to a new country every year, and this year he had taken a forty-hour train ride from Hanoi to Saigon. He is sixty-one, he says. 'Well, you have more stamina than I do,' I told him.

In my room in the Cuu Long Hotel in Vinh Long, there are some baffling notices behind the door. Over the basin there is one I understand very well; it says simply, 'No drinking'. A quite unnecessary sign; I have no intention of drinking the rust-coloured liquid that comes out of the tap when I turn it on. Behind the door, though, there are more serious instructions. 'For guarantee properties, human life and security' one says.

And it goes on to list various 'Articles':

1) Do not connecting wire or wires electricity under casual way . . .
2) Do not use electric wiring, silver paper replacing fuse . . .
3) Do not use electric wire put directly in socket.
4) Do not placing barricade on the passage.

There are other 'Do not' signs around the room here and there, all in the same strange English. All the stranger, I reflect, because many Vietnamese speak very good English. Still, I am glad to be reassured I will not find any stray barricades in the corridor.

The hotel stands on the water. On the stilts that support a terrace at the back of it, men sit with fishing rods, and the roar of motorboats fills the air. The activity is intense. Whole families are transported up and down the river in long, crowded launches with wooden awnings to keep off the noonday sun beating down on the off-white, conical hats of Vietnamese mothers, who tilt them to give shade to babies sleeping in their laps, and smaller craft with long shafts with propellers on the end driven by powerful outboard engines, zoom by at great speed – craft that would be called 'dragon-boats' on the Bangkok River.

A tour of the labyrinth of narrow waterways across the river from Vinh Long was sometimes hazardous. Occasionally a rivulet was just wide enough – only just – to permit two boats to pass each other; at other times four or five bigger and more powerful boats could overtake each other, boats on which the owner and helmsman sat perched cross-legged high over the stern, often with his wife and children under an awning beside him. Many boats were so loaded with Tet flowers, usually orange chrysanthemums, that the children's heads could barely rise above them – just black fringes of hair, half-moon eyes, and palms waving nervously at us. Boys and men lounged and dozed on the decks of other large craft; and most propped themselves up to wave; so did women walking along the banks of the waterways, smiling under their mollusc hats; lines of quacking ducks paddled after each other and rooted round floating hyacinth plants for God knows what edible grubs that lived below the surface.

Once Tam and I stopped at a wooden house on the riverbank where Tam had friends and we drank hot, weak Vietnamese tea from tiny handleless cups which were brought to us by Tam's smiling friend and her four giggling daughters. Later they brought cakes – very sweet and tasting of plums; and later still, towards sunset, we walked through the garden at the back of the house; and orchards of all sorts of Vietnamese fruit trees – jackfruit and pineapples, milkfruit and red apples. It was an idyllic setting. How was it possible not to think of a famous guerrilla hero of this part of the Delta, who said, 'There is no one in the world more influenced by love than my brother the peasant'?

Soon it became quite dusky under the thick canopy of trees along the narrow waterway we were in, and at about the same time our boat-boy who had found that the propeller of the boat had come adrift, stripped to his shorts and plunged into the water to repair it. After several minutes of jumping and plunging in the muddy water, he stuck his head above the surface to say, 'If you're in a hurry, why don't you get a tow? I'll stay, repair it and join you later.'

'How long will you be?' asked Tam anxiously.

'About ten minutes,' he said grinning at us from the water.

'More than that,' I said to Tam. 'Did you see the thickness of the pin he's trying to thread through the propeller-shaft? He'll never do it.'

So we threw a rope to a passing boat and ended the day being towed back to Vinh Long through the thickening darkness.

'Thanks, Tam,' I said to tease her. 'Tam's Towed Boat Tours of the Delta, eh? You should advertise.'

'It has never happened before,' she pretended to wail. 'This is the first time. You come here and the boat breaks down.' Her laughter rang across the water and other boatloads of people began laughing, too. And so we arrived at the boat pier in a storm of laughter, and whoops of glee or derision for the boat-boy (the 'Frog-Boy', I called him) from his mates. I gave the Frog-Boy $3 for some warming tea, a quick rub with a towel, and as a sop to his hurt pride. And when we parted, we looked back, and saw him laughing and waving, as happy as anything.

We were towed westward towards the sun as it went down behind heavy cloud on the horizon. The water thrown up by a stiff breeze was steely-grey, and the river – this branch of it at least – was wide (the ferry takes ten minutes to cross it). Clumps of water hyacinth remind me of the Chao Praya at Bangkok, although here it is less dense, gathering in thin wreaths round the pillars of the Mekong's few bridges.

At one point Tam took the words out of my mouth, so to speak: 'Do you think of the war now?' she asked.

'I was just thinking about that. I was thanking God for the fact that there are no planes overhead. No clanking helicopters and no American servicemen in Vinh Long. I hope you won't let Vietnam become too Americanized, Tam.'

'That may be a problem,' she said. 'There are rather few of them now. But of course there'll be more. And Coca-Cola and whisky, and drunkenness and shouting.'

'Well, that's the sort of thing I mean. Although whisky is not confined to Americans,' I smiled, 'I like whisky too, you know.'

'I hope the government will know how to control all that.'

'So do I.'

At the Can Tho ferry, buses were waiting in line with passengers clutching boxes on their knees marked 'Chilli Sauce' and '7-Up'. The air was literally blue with petrol fumes from the buses and a mass of old motorbikes and ancient motor-cyclos which looked as though they had to be cranked up with a handle they were so old and dilapidated. When the ferry approached with the red flag of Vietnam with the yellow star on her masthead, the bus drivers climbed back into their cabs through their front windows, and the girls with trays of '777' cigarettes and chewing gum scattered in all directions.

On the subject of beggars, Tam is illuminating.

'Some crooked people,' she says, 'like to dress up as monks and hang around tourist sites. They sometimes make money, particularly from Thai people, who are generous to monks at home and don't know fake monks when they see them here.' Tam, I have noticed, is normally very generous to beggars. But there are no monks on the ferry.

Can Tho was a revelation. Naturally, it had grown much bigger in thirty years and now it has at least one boulevard with an avenue of trees that give it almost a metropolitan look. Tam was born and went to school here, and later she met her husband, Viet, at Can Tho university and they decided to go into the tourism business together. That meant moving to Ho Chi Minh City. But Tam and Viet are Delta people.

Near Tam's father's house I see stalls with glass cases full of live snakes, big and small, beady-eyed and entwined obscenely together. Next door is a similar case full of rails (small birds with sharp, protruding beaks, and inquisitive looks), and another containing a mongoose, a large python and a number of small tortoises.

We eat rice and vegetables at a noodle shop which burns joss-sticks at a small shrine in the same room, making it hard to eat since the smoke from the sticks gets into one's eyes and nose. It is very hot indeed, despite the slow-turning ceiling fan. But we are lucky to get anything to eat at all. At other noodle shops, people say, 'Nothing to eat today, sorry.' Or that the rice has not yet been cooked. Tet is difficult; like a bank holiday in Wales.

Dinner is a different matter. I am invited to go to Tam's house where I meet her father, her husband Viet, Tam's brother-in-law, her sister, and their four children. Tam's brother-in-law is a computer expert, and on a bench are scattered the component parts of various computers waiting to be assembled.

Tam's father is a charming, amusing man who clowned about with a Vietnamese guitar – a round, primitive-looking instrument with a long arm and, I think, only four strings. The sounds he made with it sounded all right to me, but other people in the room put their hands over their ears and laughed, so I suppose he was playing some Vietnamese music deliberately badly. At any rate, Tam's father is delightful and he tells me he is off to America soon. At least he will be spared the trials and agonies that beset Ho Trang's sons when they tried to leave seven years earlier.

He is, says Tam, an avid collector of old books on tradition, history, things like that. He tries to buy them from Vietnam, China, France, England – everywhere. His wife disapproves; she is always complaining, 'Oh, Tam, your father has bought such-and-such a book (or a whole collection of old books). He'll be the ruin of us!'

*

The road out of Can Tho westwards to Chau Doc – first stop: Long Xuyen – is narrow and beautiful. I have an idea it is one of the most beautiful roads in Vietnam. In fact, if I ever came to live in Vietnam, I would want to live either here or in Nha Trang. The Mekong runs close to the road and the graceful houses on its banks stand on stilts among tall flowering shrubs; the rice fields stretch away behind them like a shining emerald counterpane, and the road itself is peaceful and not overburdened with traffic.

In Long Xuyen, Tam gets out of the car and buys a good many heads of the lotus plant – they look a bit like the nozzle of a shower, but green. 'Eat the seeds,' says Tam, 'they are very good for the health. Good for the brain, if it becomes muddled and tired.'

Is she saying that lotus seeds are good for senile dementia? Is it a hint that I may have it? I look at her closely. Her expression is inscrutable; so is the smile that plays round her mouth.

In Chau Doc we pulled up at a first-class hotel – the Hông Chau – the terrace of which is broad and looks down on the Mekong. I could see the ferry from here to the island between Chau Doc and Hông Ngu – from which Bao and Ly had set out by boat towards unknown Phnom Penh one fearful morning in 1988.

It was strange being here in peacetime and as a tourist, eating breakfast, drinking tea, almost in the very place where two Vietnamese I now knew very well in totally alien circumstances had suffered unimaginable mental torture not so very long ago. It was a very different world here now to the one they had fled, feeling, as Bao had said to Mme Bong, that 'Death is better than this life'.

Of course, Bao must have had moments in the next two years when he doubted that statement because things were not to go smoothly or safely for him and Ly until the day they escaped at last from Asia – two years after what most people would have considered a lifetime of suffering.

At any rate, the two boys crossed into Cambodia (still occupied by the Vietnamese Army, by the way) by a small boat and reached Phnom Penh safely. It was on their way to Kompong Som, the Cambodian port on the Gulf of Thailand, that things turned sour.

Ly was arrested by Vietnamese soldiers on the road to the port.

I asked him later, 'Ly, what did they ask you? Where are you going and why, that sort of thing?'

He replied, 'Yes, that sort of thing; and when I was answering them I saw their officer looking at my watch and a ring I was wearing. Well, I gave them to him. And I was allowed to return to Phnom Penh by bus – Bao and the others in my group had gone on ahead, you see. In Phnom Penh I found one of the organizers of our group – she was the head of it actually, and her husband was the military officer in charge of the capital, Phnom Penh. He was very powerful, as you can imagine. Anyway, I rejoined the group in Kompong Som, thanks to him.'

And Bao? 'Bao was small; he was so scared. When I went missing, he had thought of joining me back in Phnom Penh. He felt he couldn't go on without me. But at the last moment, I showed up and we went on together. On board, that is, a boat to Thailand.'

Their boat was a strange one. It had a crew of two and flew the Khmer (Cambodian) flag but changed to the Thai flag when they approached the Thai coast.

There were about fifty-seven people on that boat, excluding the crew, said Ly. 'We sailed through a bad storm and perhaps because of this we were lucky. We saw no pirates.'

Ly was luckier than he knew. Because, unlike others, this group of Vietnamese refugees saw no Thai pirates, landed on the island of Koh Kut and spent a more or less uneventful week there with the Thai army. Then they shifted to the mainland, to a horrible camp called Lemnot without benefit of the UN or Red Cross (who were not allowed to see them). They were moved again to Banthad on the Cambodian–Thai border. Here the UN and Red Cross people were allowed in – so it was better in some ways, and in any case it was a new camp.

Ly added, in reply to a question from me, 'Yes, you bought your way out of Vietnam. One thousand dollars for each person – and officials you paid "fixed" the soldiers and police. And arranged everything.'

I have mentioned Thai pirates and Ly and Bao's luck in not meeting any. The pirates I had in mind were very real; they had been Thai fishermen originally, but a journalist has written that 'falling catches, rising fuel costs and the lure of gold of defenceless, attractive women had turned these normally law-abiding fishermen into monsters'.

To take one case this journalist mentioned: a Thai pulled one young mother by the hair from the hold of the boat where she was hiding and deliberately threw her baby son into the water to drown. Sometimes a battered sixteen-year-old girl was the sole survivor of a boatful of something like twenty-two refugees raided by pirates. Ho Trang's son No was in a refugee boat off South Vietnam when it was attacked by Thai fishermen but they were merciful, fortunately for him, and in any case he was a tough, teenage boy, not an attractive girl to be violated. Sometimes, though, it was almost as bad to be a boy as a girl; the raiders often tipped the men into the sea, holding them off at knife-point to drown, and then raped the women at their leisure, beating them up with fists, hammers and knives, before throwing *them*, too, into the water. The notorious Thai island of Koh Kra was often mentioned as a haunt of these monsters and this jungle-capped finger of rock forty miles from the coast directly on the route from Cambodia to Thailand was the scene of many atrocities.

Of course, nobody was ever caught and punished for these unspeakable activities. They were hardly reported in the press. They are one reason why I always say that to the number of Vietnamese killed or missing, military or civilian, during the long years of war, one should never forget to add the untold numbers of refugees who never returned to their country and never even reached their intended country of exile.

There are as many Vietnamese at the bottom of the Gulf of Thailand and the South China Sea as ever reached safety.

In the hotel at Chau Doc was another Vietnamese from Virginia, a *Viet Kieu* who talked to me about his escape from Vietnam five years before. He, too, had ended up in Thailand, but he had been one of the very lucky ones. He had bribed his way on to a boat that left Vietnam from Ca Mau to the southwest of where we sat. He ended up in a camp at Songkhla in Thailand ('Thank heavens!' he said). His father had been a South Vietnamese Army captain, whose last post before Saigon fell was Can Tho. Later he spent eight years in a re-education camp.

The result of that was simply that Vietnam lost the services of a lively and successful businessman. When I asked the *Viet Kieu* with me in the hotel if he supposed his father would have made a successful executive if he had stayed, or if he himself would have made one, he clenched his teeth and did not reply. Regret? Remorse?

The Victorian writer George Meredith had known what it was to ask a question and receive no response:

> Ah, what a dusty answer gets the soul
> When hot for certainties in this our life.

The road to Hông Ngu was long and difficult. We took the small two-car ferry across the wide arm of the Mekong, and then careered mile after mile, hooting frantically to clear the narrow road of motor-bikes, the occasional car, water buffaloes with their calves, dogs, and small, apparently suicidally inclined children, through villages full of people in sarongs with dark skins, and houses of wood on stilts where old men sat on the steps of their verandahs gazing at the bedlam in the road below.

At about seven o'clock in the evening we stopped the car to sit at a café table, looking across the water of Hông Ngu, and listening to the quacking, happy Vietnamese voices around us. I order a 333 beer and try to think of the terror in the breast of little Bao as he was waiting to begin the mysterious journey into the Unknown.

The flat land ran away in all directions, divided by meandering rivers of muddy water. A flight of egrets homeward-bound after their day in the paddy fields made a line of whiteness across the orange strips of cloud where the sun had just gone down. All was peaceful. Pirates, rape, and violence seemed very far away.

I ordered one more 333 and watched as a small group of Vietnamese boys drinking Coca-Cola at the next table invited a pretty waitress in an *ao dai* to sit with them and she accepted.

That evening the air was heavy with unshed rain. The head waiter serving dinner at the hotel told me that he is twenty-eight years old and that he will marry the girl cashier in five months' time. The bride price, he said with something like pride, was very high. Was she worth it? 'Oh, yes,' he said. 'We Vietnamese like to be married.'

Next day we returned to Saigon. It was quite a strenuous drive; although there was a heavy shower of rain at My Tho, we got back in time for a late lunch. That afternoon, I thought of Coca-Cola, bride prices and weddings, as I lay on my bed in the Asian Hotel. No one had tried to arrest me, as they had arrested poor Ly, and no one had cast envious eyes on my watch or my ring. How things had changed . . .

Chapter 14

When last year I returned to Nha Trang on the coast north of Saigon after an absence of twenty-four years, I had two things in mind – both memories from a long time back, one happy, one very sad. The first thing was the finest French restaurant in the world (so it had seemed to me in 1973): the Frégate served superb fresh lobsters with beautiful French white wines. I wondered if it could still be there.

The second thing I remembered was far less pleasant, and the memory of that went further back. I have recounted the story of the little South Vietnamese soldier who died lying across my knees during a Delta skirmish in another book. But the essentials will bear repeating.

The action occurred south of My Tho, I remember, in the Mekong Delta. I was walking in a single file of South Vietnamese soldiers along one of the narrow banks that divided the paddy fields covering the land in every direction. At one moment I found myself walking alongside a young Vietnamese soldier who said to me, pointing to my boots which happened to be suede, 'Shoes you, number one.'

I told him I would give them to him when this operation was over, but he said, 'Oh, no. You very big. Small me', and after a little while he asked me if I came from America.

'No,' I replied, 'from England.'

'Home me, Nha Trang,' he went on. And later he said, 'You number one friend. Come Nha Trang, okay?'

I said I would like to come to his home in Nha Trang very much. And I would have. But fate ruled otherwise.

Presently, as we approached a tree line in a sudden rain storm, a shell burst amongst us. It was as if it had sprung out of the ground and not fallen from the sky at all. I was thrown to the ground by the blast and lay there waiting for other shells to finish us off. But luckily it turned out to be a brief ambush not a sustained harassment. A heavy silence fell. My hands shook and my heart thumped, and I heard a strange human sound quite close to me; half-sob, half-gasp. A helmet lay on the ground like an abandoned sea shell and near it lay my new friend from Nha Trang. He was clasping his stomach with one hand, and pushing feebly at the ground with the other. He was trying to get up. I went over and stopped him.

Then I put my left hand round his shoulders and made him lean back across my knees. I didn't know what to do next. His eyes were screwed up, and rain poured down his face, and I suddenly was aware of a terrible smell. I opened his sodden shirt, I remember, and saw that below his breast bone was nothing but a dark, shining mess – ripped clothing stained with rain, blood, bile and whatever comes out of bellies torn open by metal splinters.

His eyes flickered open after a bit and he frowned. 'Hurt me,' he said faintly.

He was dying. I knew that at least. He fumbled for my right hand – in a futile way I had been trying to wipe the rain from his face – and pressed it to the warm liquid mass where his stomach had been. I remember that very clearly – and I also remember that, although I am normally rather squeamish, I didn't feel the least disgust. I had a crazy idea that between us we might hold him together.

'Hurt me,' he whispered again. At the corner of the delicate half-moon fold of his eyelid a drop of water had lodged. Rain? A tear? I had no idea.

I started babbling. 'I go your home, we go stay your home, see your mother and brothers, you so much my friend. Oh Christ,' I thought, 'help him. What the hell am I doing here? God and Jesus help him –

help me – I go your home if you live – you must *live* – you my number one friend. I give you my shoes – everything.'

Someone – I don't know who – touched my shoulder and said, 'Right then. Let's take him away.' I don't remember what I replied. But the next thing, whoever it was said, 'Okay, skip it, bud. We'll be back. Take it easy.'

The tear was still there. So was the smell. I saw the delicate lip and fine hairs at the corner of the mouth. The delicate line of jaw and cheek and eyelid. I saw the mud, the grime, and the blood. I smelt the stench. I heard the pain in 'Ooooh', as his mouth opened and the upper lip rose. I felt his hand tighten on my neck, then fall slowly away, down my shoulder, arm and elbow, and down at last to the wet earth. The little body was quite limp now. The mouth a little open, showing the tips of tiny white teeth. He was dead.

I remember feeling this was the end of everything. There was nothing else to do. There was no point in moving; one might as well stay here for ever.

Soon people came and carefully lifted him up and carried him away. He was completely limp, I remember, and his head lolled back as if a hinge in his neck had snapped. I was left stunned, with my hands and clothes stinking of an abattoir.

Naturally, when I went to Nha Trang many years later – although the war was still on – I could not trace my dead friend. I hadn't even had time to ask him his name.

But when I returned last year the Frégate was still there. I stayed there for old times' sake. It was no longer a wonderful French restaurant, of course. Wholly transformed, it was now a government hotel called Thang Loi: cheap, with big modern annexes of rooms, and a restaurant which catered mostly to vociferous weekend parties of Vietnamese tourists from Saigon and which displayed a menu in which nearly half the dishes were written in Russian. I learned from an old waiter who had worked there for many years that, after 1975, Russian engineers from the base at Cam Ranh Bay down the coast had frequented the Frégate until the late 1980s. In those penurious days there was only Vietnamese vodka to drink, very strong stuff, costing only $1.50 a bottle so that a glass of it cost about 25 cents in American money – nothing, really. The lobsters and the French white wines had gone.

Native Land
by Giang Nam

When I was a boy and to school went twice a day
I loved my native land through what books had to say.
'Who says a buffalo-boy leads a hard life?'
Dreaming, I listened to the birds that sang on high,
Often played truant,
Catching, near the pond, the butterfly,
And was caught myself by Mama . . .

The girl next door looked at me, and giggled . . .
Then the Revolution broke out,
And the long war began . . .

Today I heard of you.
How hard to think! Yet, it's true . . .
They shot you and threw you away.
Why? 'You're a partisan,' they say.
I once loved my native land for its birds and butterflies,
For the days when I played truant:
I love it now, for on each clod of earth there lies
Part of the flesh and blood of the girl I'll love for ever.

The author of this poem – or the part of it I have quoted above – is a sixty-seven-year-old Vietnamese called Giang Nam, who lives in Nha Trang where he was born, and whom I met at the Association of Writers and Artists there.

The Association is controlled by the communist government in Hanoi so its members are hardly impartial Vietnamese writers and artists. For example, their view of Bao Ninh, the author of *The Sorrow of War* – a novel I have quoted from several times in this book because I believe Bao Ninh to be sincere – is that he should not have spilt the beans about the trials and horrors, the official lies told them and the official deceptions practised for political reasons on the Northern soldiers in the war with the Americans. Perhaps a good deal of the hostility the writers of Nha Trang professed towards Bao Ninh was simply based on jealousy: after all, he had had a great international success; they had not. But I may be wrong about that.

What I do know is that Giang Nam is a delightful person, whose poem *Native Land*, though well known to all Vietnamese because it is taught in every school throughout the country, is not as well translated into English, I suspect, as it might be. It had made no money for its author because the Hanoi government does not believe in paying good money for works of written composition – of any kind.

Nevertheless Giang Nam is a jolly individual. He came to the Frégate the first time I had returned there with two writer compatriots, Do Kim Cuong and another poet, Dao Xuan Quy, from the same Association, and later I invited him to come again, because I wanted to have a copy of his poem in its English version. His short, merry form appeared at my hotel bang on time, and he brought me not only the poem in English, but also flourished at me a photograph of himself at work, saying, 'Well, I thought you might like this as a souvenir, M. Young.' We talked together in French, which he spoke much better than English.

Neither of his friends had been translated, I believe, into French or English, although Cuong had written no fewer than ten novels about his wartime experiences, and none of them thought much of Bao Ninh. Now Giang Nam gave me a copy of a year-old edition of *Geo* magazine in French which forecast that Vietnam would be an economic success in twenty years' time, if it kept on going as it was going at present.

I asked Giang Nam whether he agreed with that assessment or if he thought, as some people said they did, that Vietnam was going back to the state it was in in that terrible year 1985. He said he doubted it: it was too late to go back. The 'people' would not allow it. He agreed with me that it was a pity Uncle Ho was not still alive because the corruption was getting worse and worse. He said he sometimes argues, at the provincial level, against some of the iniquities of the political cadres but doubted if his advice is much heeded.

I cited Ho Chi Minh's words – spoken as long ago as 1946 – warning against corruption, nepotism, favouritism and arrogance. All things, Ho said, which can make the people hate the government.

'You are very direct, Mr Young,' Giang Nam said, smiling. 'I admire you for that.'

'Well,' I said, 'life is too short, Mr Giang Nam, for anything else, isn't it?'

'You know, Mr Cuong, Mr Quy and I agree with that,' he said.

I liked Giang Nam; he is a good-hearted, humorous man. Although his colleagues might agree with me, I somehow doubted that they would say so in public.

The first time I visited Nha Trang in 1973, during the war, a Dr Thach told me his medical journals were continually being stolen by the post office people who re-sold them to other doctors. Someone else told me, 'We must overcome our inhibitions about the communists.' (What inhibitions were those?) He called any international intervention to end the war 'irrelevant'. All depends on Vietnamese goodwill, he said. Had he but known it, there was little enough of that to spare.

*

It was strangely apropos my meeting with Giang Nam that shortly after it I read that a panel of expatriate managers had got together and decided that Vietnam was the most stressful Asian country to work in. The main cause of the stress in doing business in Vietnam (and China, incidentally) was said to be an 'initial inability to communicate and understand each other's specific goals for joint ventures' and, once an agreement was entered into, 'a continued inability to communicate each other's logic and concerns', and the glaring reason, I knew, was corruption, particularly in the realm of customs clearance.

This was something that the Central Committee of the Communist Party of Vietnam was continually waging war against. 'The struggle against wastefulness, high-handedness, harassment and all other illegal activities must be waged with firmness and persistence', communiqués from Hanoi regularly warned.

The Vietnamese themselves, typically, told amusing stories about their own 'stressful' peccadillos. One went as follows: A foreign pig and a Vietnamese hen agreed to form a joint venture together to produce Ham 'n' Eggs. They discussed the matter at length and were getting close to agreeing on the form of the joint venture. But suddenly the foreign pig jumped up, shouting, 'Hey, wait a minute! You realize, I suppose, that when this project gets off the ground I shall be dead. I, I suddenly realize, am the *Ham*!' The Vietnamese hen chuckled. 'Well, this is a joint venture, isn't it?' she said innocently. 'Somebody has to suffer. And it isn't going to be the Vietnamese, is it?' Remember, a *Vietnamese* told me that story.

Nha Trang lies on a beautiful bay skirting the sea. You could say it is the French Riviera of Vietnam in the summer, when the fishing boats are at sea among the islands and the tourist boats scull about ferrying visitors from abroad – or even from Saigon or Danang – from Nha Trang's little port to the islands that lie slumbering like porpoises in the sun across the blue bay.

There is a war memorial at one end of the seaside corniche. 'The People will remember you,' it says. But the war and those who died in it (the 'wavering band') are half-forgotten already, like the dead on the First and Second World War memorials in British and French villages today. The living prefer to forget the horrors of war once they are free of them.

The poor want to concentrate on earning a living. Can they live on what they're earning – that is their prime concern. Salaries are low in Vietnam. A barmaid in the Century Hotel in Hué says she is paid $28 a month – with tips that comes to perhaps $30, she says. Thanh, a receptionist, gets $30 a month plus tips (which are meagre). Ha, the driver of Hué, gets $50 a month. Once a month he manages to pay a local prostitute $5 for a 'short time (with condom)'. Quoc, a waiter, gets only $20 a month. He wants to get another, better-paying job. His father is seventy-one, his mother is also seventy-one and earns a further $15 a month from her market stall, his elder sister is twenty-two, one brother is a schoolboy aged nineteen, another brother is only fifteen, and he has a tiny sister of about five or six. Quoc's house is very simple. It has a shaggy, leafy roof and walls, a large Buddhist shrine with candles, one huge cupboard, two or three beds, an open kitchen. The house is hot despite an electric fan, and there are mosquitoes. It has mats on the floor where it is not plain mud. No radio, no TV. 'Does the rain come in?' I ask. 'Oh, yes,' says Quoc. 'Often.'

When I gave Quoc $100, he immediately passed it on to his father. A good thing is that family ties are still very strong in Vietnam.

In Nha Trang, as around Quoc's house in Hué, thin, almost hairless dogs scratch their bare flanks at the roadside. Here – and even more in Hué – some side streets have tumbledown near-hovels like Quoc's house, standing next door to smartly pillared houses or newish-looking hotels. How come? The contrast is extraordinary; but also somehow interesting architecturally.

*

It is a harsh thing to have to face the fact that Minh and Qué and all their families, having been as purely 'Vietnamese' as Ha and Quoc at one time (they all were born in Hué, after all) will now be *Viet Kieu* and in all probability will never be anything else. *Viet Kieu* are immediately distinguishable from ordinary Vietnamese by their garish Western clothes and – if they have been exiles for a long time – by their sometimes rather arrogant display of money.

There is a typical *Viet Kieu* here in Nha Trang. He is about forty and owns a bar on the beach. It is a good, honest bar and he has taken trouble to decorate his Log Bar (as he calls it) with imagination and the use of skilled local Vietnamese wood carvers. He is a pleasant person, and one can't help admiring him. He has changed his name from Do Ngo to Don Ango simply by adding an 'n' to the Do and an 'a' to the Ngo; a neat trick. The ordinary Vietnamese who have stayed on view the *Viet Kieu* with 'esteem, envy or contempt', as an American observer has said, depending on their behaviour. But Don Ango, I believe, is to be thanked for providing jobs and improving the beach scene. He is a typical *Viet Kieu*, judging by his clothes: long, knee-length, baggy white shorts, and a garish T-shirt with short sleeves. He has made a shrewd point of getting to know Nha Trang's Governor: a wise move.

The average Vietnamese, although very poor, manages to keep himself spotless, he wears neat cheap trousers and shirts, usually with the sleeves rolled up. One dreads the day, if it comes, when he will slop about like a scruffy Western teenager (there are plenty of backpackers in Vietnam setting the tone) in a long T-shirt covering his knees and floppy cotton 'shorts' that reach down to his calves, and matted shoulder-length hair.

That said, one must add that if the Hanoi government had enlisted the knowledge and know-how of many more Vietnamese after their victory in 1975 there would not now be so many intelligent *Viet Kieu* missing from the country, and it is very possible that the economy of Vietnam would be in a better state than it is.

Young Dung is certainly not a *Viet Kieu*. He works at the Tranh The restaurant owned by Mr Duc and his wife Chi, whose little place sells fair Vietnamese food at reasonable prices. The restaurant is usually full, so I suppose they do good business. Dung, when he is not giggling as he serves in the restaurant, drives me to Don Ango's Log Bar every evening on Duc's small Honda motorbike. Sometimes, too, he drives me out in the morning to Hon Chong, a rocky headland overlooking a long curving bay with a ring of trees with rooftops showing through them, and a small island off the coast with a pagoda on it on which a solitary monk is said to live. Dung drives too fast, of course; he should be a fighter pilot. So our journey to Hon Chong is rapid but fraught.

One day, as we stopped here, Dung said: 'Monk? How do you write that?'

I said, 'Simple. M-O-N-K. Like "monkey" without the -ey.'

I didn't know what I had started. Pandemonium broke out. Dung thought that was hilarious, at least the funniest thing he had ever heard. He began to chant at the top of his voice, 'Monkey! Monkey!'

I shouted at him, 'No, Dung, not monkey! *Monk!*'

But he was giggling so hysterically he could not hear me.

'Buffalo,' I yelled at him, using a mild insult, '*Viet bac!*' (North Vietnamese). Dung came from Hanoi originally.

'No,' he spluttered. 'Me Viet Cong.'

'Rubbish. You're too young. Buffalo!'

I certainly couldn't have him going about insulting harmless monks by shouting 'monkey' at them, could I?

Quite often I can't help thinking of the little soldier from Nha Trang killed across my knees thirty-odd years ago. He would be about fifty now, I suppose, and might be wearing a version of my suede boots if he were still alive. I would dine with his family from time to time, of course, because I am sure he would invite me. 'You friend number one,' he had said. He might own a small restaurant . . .

But all I could really remember was his murmured 'Hurt, me' . . .

And remembering him sometimes spoils my enjoyment of this beautiful place.

Chapter 15

In 1996 I returned to Hanoi to see if I could find any clues to the character of the man who had won the epic struggle for Vietnam's independence, the man who, with his goatee beard, for many years must have reminded many in the West of the fictional villain of Sax Rohmer's novels about Dr Fu Manchu.

Ho Chi Minh (born Nguyen Ai Quoc in 1890) has also been described as a 'man as pure as Lucifer', as Gandhi, as Mr Chips. Uncle Ho had the misfortune to die in 1969, just as the great dream of his life was about to be realized. He had captured the imagination of the Western world years before by then, as obviously he had captured the hearts and minds of his followers.

'If free elections were held in Tongking,' said an article in *Paris Match* in 1952 (that could have been written in 1965), 'Ho Chi Minh would receive 70 per cent of the vote. His face is the most familiar one in the whole world of Indo-China, as familiar to everyone, peasant or intellectual, as Stalin or Winston Churchill are in the West.'

On top of that, the article went on to say, 'Ho Chi Minh's soldiers belong to the same race as those Southerners fighting with the French [substitute the word 'Americans'], but with them he has produced a courageous and disciplined force which possesses all the virtues of a revolutionary army: devotion to the cause (for many of its members a nationalist rather than a communist one), a beloved leader, officers who have moved up from the ranks (in the South Vietnamese Army too many of the indigenous officers are the sons of families of wealthy landowners who have no real affinity with the peasants they command).'

What Ho Chi Minh would think of Vietnam today is anyone's guess: would he approve of television, the mobile phones, karaoke bars, traffic jams, private hotels and all the rest? Other people than I have asked the same unanswerable question. Personally I like to think that the stern but kindly figure, giving an impression of simplicity and candour ('there was nothing evasive about him; this was a man who gave orders and expected obedience and also love') would have been tolerant of such things up to a point.

One visitor (Graham Greene) went on to say of him: 'The kind, remorseless face had no fanaticism about it . . . So much love had been given and received, so many sacrifices demanded and suffered . . . His socks flapped as he waved back at me from the doorway, telling me not to hurry, to stay as long as I liked, to have another cup of tea. I could imagine them flapping across the school quad, and I could understand the loyalty of his pupils.'

Such a man with flapping socks has no place in a mausoleum. He would suit admirably the little house by the side of a fish pond that stands across the wide road designed for goose-stepping parades and formal investitures, which I had visited once before with Mr Chuong on my first return visit in 1995. In this house half hidden in trees I felt nearer to the great man than anywhere else. It was just the sort of simple house in just the sort of simple setting of flowers and fish ponds and shady trees that would have suited him – at least would have suited the man with the familiar goatee who appeared in the postcards I had bought from the woman at the entrance of his garden: Uncle Ho loading up a horse in 1950; Uncle Ho sitting on the grass outside a straw hut full of North Vietnamese soldiers; Uncle Ho feeding fish in the pond by his house in 1960, nine years before he died.

From my hotel, a taxi driver said he could take me to Ho's house for $40 including a wait of two hours. But a friendly cyclo driver said he would do it for $2 all in, and this offer I accepted. We arrived at the end of the long road to the house and garden and a self-important policeman signalled the cyclo driver to turn and park his vehicle some way away from the place he thought of stopping. That in itself was a long way from the house; the new parking place would be even further, out of sight, in fact.

Ignoring the policeman, despite his angry cries and the intimidating blasts on his whistle, I pressed ahead (making sure that my driver was not arrested) until I came upon an official-looking man in plain clothes who might have been a detective. Whatever he was, he made no effort to stop me and in fact pointed me courteously on my way towards Ho's house and its fish pond. The man in uniform had meanwhile disappeared.

White doves swooped overhead, heading for roosts in a large barnlike house. Soldiers paraded in the road by the mausoleum. But I pressed on again, passing a few chattering tourists from Singapore or Taiwan, and arriving at last at the gates that led to the fish pond. Here all was quiet. Perfect peace surrounded the immensely tall trees, the palms, the brilliant flame-coloured blooms, the pond in which the dark shapes of fish moved like shadows. A hen wandered down the path in front of me.

Soon I came to a gap in the hedge and a short path led to the house on stilts where two sentries with rifles and white gloves stood. One of the sentries yawned as I approached, opening his mouth to what looked like its fullest extent, and behind him I saw the plain conference table ringed with chairs at which the North's war cabinet had pondered their next moves while in the later stages of the war the American B-52s rained bombs down on Hanoi. Upstairs was a study and a small bedroom with an alarm clock beside the bed. And in the study a few books stood on a kind of dressing table and beside them, incongruously, a sun helmet of khaki-green. The only thing that was missing, I thought, was a packet of English cigarettes and a lighter, or possibly a box of

Swan Vestas matches, for, ascetic though he was, Ho had one fad – he was forever pulling on an English cigarette (had he become addicted to them in the Hong Kong prison or in the kitchen of the Carlton Hotel in London?).

It was a good piece of stage setting. It was as if Ho had gone out for a minute and would return as soon as the maid had rearranged his bedclothes and his books (which she had done). It made me go out next day and buy a copy of his *Selected Writings (1920–1969)* – something I had never read before. Opening it at random I came across his Report to a Special Political Conference held in March 1964. He could have made it in 1976.

'The colonial war of aggression,' he said, 'has left our economy in a state of exhaustion.' And, he adds, one of the things not to be forgotten is that 'Vietnamese nationals living in foreign lands are always thinking of the Fatherland. Those who have returned home have *eagerly contributed their talents and energies to national construction*' (the italics are mine).

That, it struck me, could have applied to Minh and Qué – in fact, to everyone in Mme Bong's family.

Perhaps the most revealing pages are those in a report which deals with the situation just after the Second World War – in 1945.

The full title of the report by Ho Chi Minh made in 1945 was: 'To the People's Committees In The Whole Country (North, South, Centre) and At All Levels'. Evidently he considered it of great importance. And there is some tough, realistic talk in it.

For instance: 'What is of benefit to the people we must strive to do. What is harmful to them we must strive to avoid. We must love the people: they will love and respect us. I know that many of you have correctly carried out the government's policies and won the people's hearts. But others among you have committed very serious mistakes.'

These Ho described. For instance: 'Traitors whose guilt is clearly established must of course be punished, and no one can complain. But sometimes arrests are made and property confiscated out of personal enmity, causing discontent among the population.'

And again: 'Some may go so far as to divert public property to their own use, casting aside integrity and honesty. Mr Commissar rides in official cars, then his wife does, then even his children. Who is going to pay for these expenses?

'Some build their own group of followers, appoint their friends and relatives to positions for which they have no ability, shove aside people who are competent and honest but are not to their liking. They forget that this is a matter of public concern, not a private affair.'

And this above all: 'As officials, some consider themselves to be sacrosanct, and look down upon the people. Their every gesture shows them to be "mandarin revolutionaries". They fail to realize that their arrogance will lose them the people's confidence, and harm the government's prestige.'

All the above shows that Ho Chi Minh, had he lived, would by now have his work cut out to discipline corrupt and arrogant cadres, 'some of whom forget that they must work for the unity of the whole people, irrespective of age and fortune, in order to safeguard the independence of Vietnam'.

An interesting aspect of this last expression of Ho Chi Minh's concern in 1945 for his cadres' good behaviour, is that exactly the same sentiments are shared by most of the present leadership in Hanoi. Corruption and arrogance: these two faults are regularly (and rightly) attacked in the Vietnamese press or in speeches by the reformist Prime Minister, Vo Van Kiet, and other leaders connected with *doi moi* (which means literally 'our way', but has come to be known as 'renovation' and is sometimes compared to Gorbachev's *perestroika*). *Doi moi* — the introduction of which has made Vietnam such a delightful place — could equally well be translated as 'communism with a smiling face' and it seems to me that is what Uncle Ho himself would like.

Corruption, of course, is a basic attribute of Asia; in fact, Singapore is probably the only place in Southeast Asia where it doesn't exist. But it is also a well-known attribute of communism. When Asia meets communism one can expect the corruption factor to proliferate.

As long ago as 1945 Ho Chi Minh had predicted, to himself at least, that 'integrity' and correctly administered 'justice' would be major requirements of a future independent Vietnam. If enough cadres 'do not work for the unity of the whole people, irrespective of age and fortune', exactly as Ho said, poor, war-ravaged Vietnam's hoped-for rise to wealth and prosperity in the world will be doomed.

'We hope you will make progress,' said Ho in 1945. He might be repeating that wish today.

I walked back to where I left the cyclo driver and his vehicle. The uniformed policeman was nowhere to be seen and I got into the cyclo and we returned to the hotel. There I gave the driver $5 instead of the $2 he had asked for. Well, I thought, he has had a fright this morning; he might have believed he was about to be arrested.

Thinking over the incident of the cyclo driver and the policeman who wouldn't let him park, it seemed to me to make a sort of parable. How different things were now in 1996 to what they had been in 1985 when I was here being shepherded around by Mr Thai. The uniformed cop might have represented Vietnam 'then'; the sympathetic plain-clothes man who had waved me on to Uncle Ho's house was the 'now'. The latter had had the sense to realize how important it was for a foreign tourist to see the place where the saviour of Vietnam had dwelt for so long. Perhaps this anonymous guard (or guide) had realized in his heart that Ho Chi Minh was not a mummified doll under a spotlight in a Moscow-designed mausoleum, but a living spirit who haunted still the humble house on stilts; that he had inspired, and would continue to inspire this 'wavering grace of humble men' exuding truth, candour and, above all, integrity in a way no lifeless figure under lights could ever do. 'This was a man who gave orders and expected obedience and also love.' Perhaps this anonymous Vietnamese realized that what Ho Chi Minh believed in 1945, he would have believed in 1996.

'We hope you will make progress,' Ho had said. Stern, kindly, remorseless Mr Chips had spoken.

Apropos all this, while I was in Vietnam in 1995, the Central Committee of the Communist Party of Vietnam met and in the words of an official communiqué 'again stressed the imperative need to continue strengthening and improving the state apparatus'.

Law enforcement remained slack, it said, state bodies were still cumbersome and inefficient in certain areas, bureaucracy, wastefulness and corruption continued to be serious problems. Ho Chi Minh's urgent words were recalled in a passage saying that the struggle against corruption, wastefulness, high-handedness, harassment and all other illegal activities must be waged with firmness and persistence.

I remembered the report to the People's Committee of 1945.

'Mr Commissar rides in official cars, then his wife does, then even his children. Who is going to pay for these expenses?' The warning voice of Uncle Ho was again sounding urgently through the land.

I have already described how, when I first arrived back in Saigon after a ten-year gap, Qué's agonized word to summon up all that had happened here was simply, *'Pourquoi?'* – 'Why?'

The very same word had struck me the day before when, driving past the American embassy, my driver had told me that the Stars and Stripes would soon be hoisted again in the garden.

Something had happened, by obscure chance, to remind me of that terrible and confused time so long ago.

It had been twenty years since President Thieu's long speech of resignation on 21 April 1975, in which he accused the Americans of 'running away and leaving us to do the job you could not do'. What a humiliating time that had been. The wonder is that the Vietnamese-in-the-street still wants to have anything to do with us (I say 'us' because I might be American as far as the Vietnamese are concerned).

Two American officers of the American military team have said they remember well the scene inside the American embassy as 'a monstrous mess'. Vietnamese employees, hoping desperately for evacuation, milled about everywhere, and one of the American officers moved through them, deliberately lying, shouting, 'Don't worry. We're not going to leave you.' He estimated there must have still been 420 Vietnamese there. Then the order came: 'End the Vietnamese evacuation. Only Americans.' The officer made his way to the roof as if on his way to the bathroom, and not too long afterwards, evacuated, he was reunited with the other officers on the deck of the USS *Oklahoma*. 'You just saw betrayal at its worst,' he said. And he – we all – have been living with that betrayal ever since.

And then by chance, as I say, something happened.

The English-language *Vietnam News*, which was pushed under my door at the Asian Hotel every morning, one day in early May 1995 carried on an inside page an article on a new book. This book, called *In Retrospect*, was, said the writer, about to become one of the major publishing events of the year (1995). I could believe that. For the book was by none other than Robert McNamara, American Defence Secretary in the early years of the American war in Vietnam during the presidency of Lyndon Johnson. In fact, the war became known to some as 'McNamara's War' and the book's subtitle was *The Tragedy and Lessons of Vietnam*. But, as the *Vietnam News* pointed out, McNamara was not the only Secretary of Defence during that war; he ceased to hold that position as early as 1967 and there were a number of others.

'Anyway,' the article ends, 'the publication of *In Retrospect* offers a great chance to put the war behind us all. A meaningful relationship between the two countries [America and Vietnam] is long overdue.

Life is lived in the present and the future. We learn from the past, but we do not relive the past.

'The 50th anniversary of the end of World War II shows that old enemies can become close friends and allies. The US and Vietnam need to do the same.'

A few days later, Wang, the newspaper seller of the Givral coffee shop, drew my attention to a copy of the *Straits Times of Singapore* which, he said, had just arrived. In it was a full-scale review of McNamara's book under the headline 'McNamara Breaks His Silence: We Were Wrong on Vietnam'. And a quote from the book was reproduced lower down in bold type: 'We were terribly wrong. We owe it to the future generations to explain why.' The whole article by Thomas W. Lippman had been reprinted from the *Washington Post*.

'According to the book,' says the review, 'the war could and should have been avoided and should have been halted at several key junctures.' The decision point came, it said, 'when the Central Intelligence Agency delivered an exhaustive analysis saying no amount of bombing would deter North Vietnam from its objective of winning the South and that a US withdrawal would not undermine overall US security interests.' Mr McNamara ignored, the article goes on to say, a seminal event of 1965 – an anti-communist coup in Indonesia – that ought to have shown them that the 'Domino theory' (by which a communist victory anywhere in Asia would lead to a toppling of non- or anti-communist regimes elsewhere in the region like a row of dominoes which push each other down one after the other) was invalid.

The article did not go on to say that, in fact, the opposite had been the case. The communists did win in Vietnam, as we know, but so far from falling to communism the other states of Asia grew more and more prosperous and their existing regimes became better entrenched.

Meanwhile Qué's life was in ruins. And so was Minh's, for that matter.

Chapter 16

I went back to Hué twice after the nightmare visit I made in 1985 with Mr Thai. Once in 1995 (exactly ten years later) and again the next year, 1996.

The second time was just before Tet – one of the wettest, coldest Tets anyone could remember.

But things were saved by the fact that it *was* Tet: the Vietnamese always are at their best and kindest at Tet, and so when my plane landed at Danang airport, there was Mr Ha waiting with an enormous bouquet of flowers and saying, with a broad grin, 'Welcome back, Pappa.'

I had met Mr Ha the year before when he had driven over the familiar old road between Danang and Hué in his rentable Toyota with the Johnnie Walker Black Label sign on the dashboard. We had done quite a lot of exploring the year before, Ha and I: we had started by going to Quang Tri. Or rather to the ruins of that town, which was levelled by the North Vietnamese Army and the Americans between them in the North's lightning invasion down the coastal plain in 1972 – the time I have described when I was caught on this very road and only got back to Hué by the skin of my teeth to find the market in flames, tipsy cyclo drivers fighting at the door of Mme Bong's house, and terrified, drunken soldiers shedding their uniforms as fast as they could and their weapons as well, after firing whole magazines into the night air.

It had been a dangerous time, and I was lucky to have made it across the bridge and found refuge in one of the modern hotels on the other side of the river, in what is now the Century Inn or the Perfume River Hotel. I had consumed the best part of a bottle of whisky that night on my own, in a blue funk, sitting in my room listening to the shots outside, waiting for the Viet Cong to burst in and finish me off.

It was not something I was proud of, and I don't think I told Mr Ha about that hotel episode, or of the sinister young receptionist who in the morning smirked at me, 'So they no come?'

There was nothing sinister about twenty-four-year-old Ha. He and I sat in the main street of Quang Tri, this town the war had destroyed twenty years ago and that no one had bothered to rebuild. All that was to be seen here now were two lines of jerry-built shops and noodle-stalls, at one of which we ordered coffee and condensed milk because that seemed to be all there was. Ha sat bolt upright, alert and inquisitive under his helmet of black hair, although he had rather sad eyes. On the way back to Hué he informed me that one thing he craved was a pair of sunglasses to drive in. So at a shop very near Mme Bong's old house, just before the big market which replaced the one that had been burned down, Ha bought the glasses which I paid for and was very pleased with himself and with me.

'You must come to my home, Pappa,' he said. 'Come to dinner. Tomorrow?'

'With great pleasure, Ha,' I said. 'Thank you.'

Some time later, Ha said, 'You know something, Pappa? If this car was mine I would drive you all over Vietnam for nothing.'

He is a good and careful driver but, alas, the car does *not* belong to him but to a company. Nevertheless, I felt a surge of affection for Vietnamese who could say something like this and obviously mean it.

'Are you happy, Ha?' I ask him.

His face lit up at once. 'Oh, yes, Pappa. I am very happy when I work!' Ha earns $50 a month. 'I am very happy if I work.'

'You are quite right, Ha. If we don't work we die. You agree?'

'Oh, yes,' he said, nodding vigorously.

At the offices on the river of the Hué Association of Writers and Artists I met a poet, Vo Que. He seemed a gentle, pleasant man of, say, forty-eight. He had written a rather well-known poem called 'The Baby Prisoner' and he gave me a copy of it now. While we were sitting round a table drinking weak Vietnamese tea from tiny cups, Vo Que told me he had been a soldier in Hué during Tet 1968, the year the communists came in and were bombed out by the Americans.

'Was there any chance of peace negotiations succeeding then?' I wanted to know how the North had viewed the Buddhist efforts to secure peace in 1966 or 1967.

'Saigon would not agree,' said Vo Que.

'But *could* negotiations have been successful?'

I couldn't expect a serious answer; nor did I get one. 'There were people,' he said, 'Americans in particular, who would not let Hué or Danang go unpunished.'

The introduction to 'The Baby Prisoner' said: 'Many small children were part of a boatload of 1,000 prisoners destined for Non Son Island [off the south coast] in May 1972. These children ranged in age from infancy to eleven years. They had to follow their families to the Island to live the life of prisoners.' Vo Que, author of 'The Baby Prisoner', was on that ship and wrote the poem during the journey. The poem followed:

The Baby Prisoner
by Vo Que

You have been in prison
                          since birth.
In the arms of Mother
                  you look like a tiny red mouse.
Prison has forced you to live a slave's life.
But Mother has taught you
                    the power of your homeland . . .

I asked Vo Que another question: 'You were a student here during the Tet Offensive in 1968. So when the North Vietnamese asked you to go away with them, did you go?'

'I didn't,' he said, shaking his head. 'I had my exams to consider.' It was a non-answer: as if Bao or Ly had refused to risk their lives to leave the country 'because they had exams to pass'.

Vo Que passed me a recent programme issued by the American Smithsonian Associates; a programme of the traditional music of Hué that had been given in the Carmichael Auditorium of the National Museum of American History. It said that the Perfume River Traditional Ensemble was led by Mr Vo Que, noted singer, poet and songwriter. There would be, the programme added, a Meet the Artist picnic the following day.

I soon moved my hotel, leaving the expensive Century where, at this very cold time of year, there was no heating whatsoever in the rooms. That seems inexcusable in an expensive hotel of this sort, and the General Manager, Peter Martin, agrees; but there is nothing he can do. In any case, he can't wait to leave. I hear Hué people are a little like the English. They think hotel, bar or restaurant work is beneath them.

So I moved across the road from the great modern block to a 'mini-hotel' immediately opposite. There I was happy. From my second-floor room I could look down Le Loi Street and see the river and even see the big flagpole on the citadel with the huge red flag with its single yellow star flying from it.

In the very simple lobby of the Trang Tien Hotel sat Mr Thanh, the receptionist, who speaks good English and who for two years was in the Vietnamese army on the Chinese border. Thanh showed me a photograph, a bit battered by now from much display, of himself dressed as a gunner of a T-54 tank in a belted tank-coat, a turned-up woolly cap with the yellow star of Vietnam on the front of it and heavily padded earflaps. Thanh has got a sharp little face and beady eyes, and in the photo he looked a very tough guy indeed, sheltered as he was under the huge cannon and the tank tracks of his immense vehicle. In reality Thanh proved to be a good and staunch friend to me and I took him with me and Ha when we visited Danang together later on. He lives in Hué with his father, but he has friends (and I suspect numerous girlfriends) in Danang. For Tet this year, I gave Thanh a box of twenty-four cans of Huda beer, the beer Tuborg, I think, make now in Hué.

From my second-floor window I noticed for the first time the sinister appearance of the elderly cyclo drivers who cluster in the street below when it rains. When the showers start the drivers pull up rain-proof screens over their vehicles and huge floppy macintosh capes with deep hoods over their own skinny bodies, so that when they shout, 'Hey, you!' they seem to be calling from the dark depths of glistening cowls. Because they become like so many images of death, you have the unpleasant feeling that the Grim Reaper has caught up with you at last.

This year there was nothing to stop me walking across the girder bridge of Trang Tien to visit Mme Bong's old house at 103 Tran Hung Dao Street.

The trouble was that the house was sadly not the same. The cubicles on the street in which the boy-tailors had busily sewed and stitched when Mme Bong lived here, had gone, replaced by the counters of watch and TV sellers. Apart from that, when I walked into the main body of the house I found that the main downstairs room – the room we always used to sit and eat in, the room with the table from which Mimi, the dog, had seized the chicken, with the derelict motorbike in the corner – had been divided into two rooms by a new wall, so that the stairs to the upper floor had mysteriously vanished. The small mortar crater had vanished, too.

But things could have been worse.

While I was standing at the entrance of No. 103, a good-looking elderly woman whose face seemed faintly familiar, approached me and made excited signs that she knew me. She also signalled to me to follow her and, not knowing what she wanted, I could only obey.

Up the street she hurried, every now and then stopping to beckon me to hurry up and follow her closely. At the end of the street we turned a sharp corner and she plunged, still mysteriously beckoning me on, down a side street full of garbage and knots of people squatting at their front doors, chatting to friends. Finally we arrived at the door of a house smaller than the rest, and the woman threw open the door.

In a crowded room stood a man of about fifty, and despite his greying hair I recognized Thien, Mme Bong's nephew – the one who years before had deserted from the South Vietnamese paratroopers in Laos by clinging to the undercarriage of a helicopter. The man who had cursed the Americans. He was living in penury now. The woman who had led me here was his wife Chi. And he introduced me to a young man in his mid-twenties, saying this was his son, Dat. In a moment or two, after much handshaking and back-thumping – it was more than twenty years since I had seen Thien and Chi – Thien delved into a trouser pocket and proudly produced a letter in Mme Bong's unmistakable hand. It was dated quite recently and asked Thien to come to Saigon as soon as possible to look after her; Phuc, Qué's surviving brother, would come to Hué at any moment. She asked Chi and Dat to take Phuc and myself to visit the tomb of her son Van. Luckily they knew exactly where it was; among all those graves it would have taken me a year to identify that particular one; there were so many.

What a coincidence, Thien said with much laughter and asked me where I was staying. I told him and he said he knew the Trang Tien Hotel well. Chi and Dat would pick me up there as soon as Phuc arrived from Saigon.

Phuc arrived next day and came to my hotel with Chi and Dat. I had arranged with Ha that he should drive us to Nui Binh, the hill of tombs. Arriving at the hill, we followed Dat at a brisk walk over a rise on the hillside and zigzagged our way between countless graves, some simple affairs shaped like lotus flowers and surrounded by cement walls arranged in horseshoe shapes. The graves covered the hillside and it would have taken me an age to have found Van's tomb on my own. To be here at night among the buried dead would have been creepy; now, under bright sun, and while small boys gambolled about the graves and raced giggling up the muddy footpaths that snaked between them, it was a fairly cheerful place. At last we came to Van's tomb; and it was like all the others. Certainly smaller than I remembered it from 1973.

Phuc said, 'I think the old tomb was grander.'

'It was,' I told him. 'Why was it changed?'

'The communists moved it – in the early 1980s, I think. And probably Mme Bong did not want to re-create it exactly. At the time the communists were against making a Southern military man's tomb look too grand.'

That must have been it, I thought. The old tomb certainly had been grander – quite different to this nondescript affair at our feet. Even the inscription was barely legible. I think it said: Tran Dinh Van – and Mme Bong's name was mentioned, and that of Minh, Van's brother, and his son Vu. But I couldn't see the year of Van's death – which was 1967 – mentioned anywhere.

It only remained to pay Ha and tip Dat with five dollars and drive back to Hué.

Mme Bong had had a hard life all right: her husband died young; her eldest son died young and her daughter died young. Throw in Tet 1968, the surrender of 1975, the seven years of Minh's imprisonment, and finally Minh's exile in America: doesn't that deserve to be called a hard life?

With Phuc I visited the citadel once again, the throne room with its playful dragons gambolling on the roof, the deep stone gates with the marks of shrapnel still on them, the huge flag waving victoriously from the principal entrance, and the missing chunks of wall where in 1968 the bombs had fallen.

'I used to play football there. I was ten years old,' said Phuc, pointing to a patch of grass inside the citadel wall which was now full of rusting tanks and guns, and had evidently once been a playing field – and maybe would be again in time.

Then we walked slowly up the road to the door of No. 103, not talking; deep, I suppose, in thoughts of the past. At Mme Bong's doorway, where Phuc's father used to roll his cigarettes, we stopped for a little while, and then crossed to the market where I bought ten gladioli for $1.75 to present to the hotel for Tet, and a mixture of roses and daisies for Phuc to take home to Thien's house.

We called it a day then, and I wandered back across the bridge to the hotel.

When I went to the DMZ Bar next to the Trang Tien Hotel that night, the endlessly repeated refrain of a pop song poured out of a jukebox, something about wanting it all and wanting it *now*.

*

People were predicting the closure of this bar, although it was harmless and I liked the owner, who said to me now: 'You look sad. Why do you look so sad?' He paused and then added, 'Did you go to the Nui Binh grave today?'

'Yes,' I said. A few days before I had told him I had hoped to go to visit Van's grave.

'Oh, I see,' he said in an understanding tone of voice. He hadn't known Van or Mme Bong, but he knew . . .

And all of a sudden I wanted a whisky.

'A Famous Grouse, please,' I said to him.

Ha arranged for another driver from his company to take me to his house for dinner. The house was near the Tu Dam pagoda which I had visited one very hot day years ago with Minh and Qué to see Thich Tri Quang. The road crosses a railway line nearby and Ha's house is on a bank overlooking the line.

His father, who comes from Hanoi and speaks a little French, offered me whisky. He explained it was from the Philippines, but from the label I saw it came from Cambodia. Cambodian whisky: I'd never heard of that before! Ha's father took three small glasses neat. I sipped it and found, as I suspected, that it is pure firewater. I got through two small glasses with water chasers. The other people in the room were Ha's mother, his girlfriend and his sister. His girlfriend bravely took a single glass of the whisky, made a terrible face, and after a little while, to my delight, her cheeks turned bright red. She is rather fat in the face, so when her cheeks turned red it made a difference – although not nearly as fat as Ha's sister, who is distinctly chubby. Ha, on the other hand, is decidedly thin.

The dinner Ha's girlfriend and his sister produced was substantial: three bowls of hot soup, cold meat cut up on four plates, bread, and vegetables and chicken in a stew. I ate very little, as usual.

Ha has told me that he earned a mere $50 a month, yet his house had four good-sized rooms. On one wall was a large picture of a waterfall, and on another a silky rug decorated with stags wandering between pine trees. Elsewhere there were lacquer vases, and in the bedroom a Honda Dream motorbike, partly hidden by a dust sheet, looked new.

The Danang–Hanoi express train rumbled past as we sat eating, its approach signalled by a strange thin hooting like a child that has lost its way, and the carriages came rattling past, and shaking the walls of the little house which stood next to and slightly above the rails. If it went by in the night too often sleep would be impossible, I said.

'Oh, we get used to it,' said Ha.

'I should think children and even adults get crushed to death sometimes on the railway line?'

'Only dogs, sometimes, Pappa. One gets used to that, too. Well, we've lived here ever since I was born. About twenty-four years, that is. No one has been killed here yet.'

'You were born here?'

'Well, I was born in hospital, actually,' said Ha, laughing.

A dog barked and a man guffawed in the trees on the other side of the railway line. Sitting on the sofa again after the meal, drinking unsweetened tea from the little cups without handles, I felt again an old affection for the Vietnamese, for the people of Hué, who had suffered so much in the war. They were poor, and yet, without thinking about it, somehow retained their dignity, generosity and humour.

There's one mass grave site in Hué: at Gia Hoi, in the garden of the secondary school there, where Vietnamese civilians caught in the Tet Offensive in 1968 had been marched to their deaths with their hands tied behind them. At this school was the only time and place that I ever heard used in the New Vietnam those typically communist words, 'Do you have permission to be here?' These threatening words assailed my ears for the first and last time in two years. Looking for the headmaster,

I had penetrated into the watchman's room at the gate and there someone had pointed out to me an English-speaking teacher – a tall, skeletal, poorly dressed man to whom I said, 'Are there many ghosts around here? Do they worry your pupils?'

Then it came: I think he narrowed his eyes to say, 'Do you have permission to be here?'

I think I replied boldly, 'I don't need permission to be anywhere.'

'You should get the director's permission to be here,' he said.

I didn't bother to explain that I had been looking for the director all along. By now I know the voice of communist authority when I hear it. I felt only shock and anger. I left without looking back.

Vo Que was right in a way when he said later, 'War can kill anybody, everybody and anywhere.' True; but it is simple murder if the killing is organized as it was in the case of the massacre of Vietnamese by Americans under Lieutenant Calley at My Lai, or at Gia Hoi – or in Bosnia, for that matter. Think, for example, of the monstrous Pol Pot in Cambodia, and his Killing Fields, of which the Vietnamese, quite rightly, so disapproved.

To banish gloomy thoughts of death, Hué's streets were full of cyclos carrying orange trees and branches of peach blossom. Quite a few car boots, too, overflowed with flowering shrubs, usually the Tet colour, yellow. It was cloudy yet the rain held off for the day. Ha drove Thanh and me to Danang (they wanted to buy Tet presents there). A strong wind blew the Vietnamese flags at my hotel door straight out from left to right.

I was sitting beside Ha as he drove past the turning to Hué's Phu Bai airport. 'What do you call that?' Thanh asked suddenly, pointing to a pillbox in the middle of a paddy field.

'A pillbox, Thanh.'

'Oh yes. Pillbo'.'

'No, Thanh. Not pillbo', pill*box*.' I emphasized the 'box'.

I said: 'Do you know, I have lost count of the number of times I landed at Phu Bai on that short strip in an Air Vietnam DC-6. Driving out of the airport and through the village near it, I would never have been surprised by a burst of machine-gun fire past my head or straight into my chest.'

Ha, his eyes on the road ahead, smiled sadly.

Thanh, in the back seat behind us, said, 'You were lucky. You are alive.'

'You and Ha are the really lucky ones. You were not born then.'

Thanh laughed and I felt his comforting hand briefly squeezing my shoulder.

Hué and Tet was alive with a springtime feeling of carefree gaiety. Flowers were everywhere; street stalls displayed everything from paintings to the famous Hué blue and white porcelain.

No one wanted to think of war, still less talk about it. And yet a good many people must have been aware of all the tragedies of that seemingly endless war. How could they not have been?

One of the older barmaids at an hotel told me that her father had been killed in the street on the first day of Tet 1968. Another, sadly shaking her head, said she knew of the massacres of Gia Hoi and Con Hen island. All sorts of people lost relatives and friends – a father here, an uncle, a great-uncle or a brother there. The father of an employee at the Trang Tien Hotel was a lieutenant in the army and did one and a half years in a hard labour camp. Yet there is no bitterness in him that I can see. No sign of a desire for revenge at all.

Vo Que had said, 'There are always killings in a war.' Perhaps that is the hideous truth that explains the lack of bitterness, the calm that pervades Annam now – and the rest of the country, for that matter.

I was flying to Saigon next day.

In the late afternoon I took a last walk from my hotel to the bridge over the Perfume River, the girdered one called Trang Tien. I leaned on the rail for a long time watching the evening light fade on the surface of the water. I looked around me at the sampans that huddled round the bridge that led to Gia Hoi; at the encircling enemy hills where once the gunfire had lit up the horizon like summer lightning. I could just see Tran Hung Dao Street (but not quite No. 103) and the cinema outside which I had first met Minh with his friend Vua all those years ago; and a little further on I could see the citadel flaunting its scars and the red flag of communist Vietnam on the river bank.

This river meant so much; it was where Minh and Qué had said farewell to the golden opportunities of their youth before they joined the war.

It was where many years ago I thought I had discovered – and knew I had fallen in love with – this enchanting country.

Chapter 17

I left Saigon – and Vietnam – at last, a few days after my birthday, 24 April 1996. On that day I woke up at the Asian Hotel to find an envelope and a small packet under my door. The packet contained a tie and a tiny ballpoint pen; the envelope contained a card with a hand-drawn picture of a small Vietnamese boy astride a water buffalo and a river with a man paddling in a sampan. An inscription inside the card read: 'Happy birthday to Dady [*sic*]! . . . Wishing All the best to you and your family.' It was signed, 'Your son! Tran Cao Dien'.

It seemed to me to sum up the friendly side of Vietnam and Saigon, and indeed Vietnamese in general, past and present. It made me even more sorry to be leaving. I had not consciously known Dien very well: his had been one friendly face among several others behind the hotel bar or serving meals in the restaurant. Nevertheless, he had made it his business to discover the date of my birthday and to go out and buy, from his slender savings, a tie, a pen and the card.

I went out into the street, saddened and elated at the same time, and saw Wang sprinting up the pavement to meet me. He had somehow heard (had I told him?) that I was leaving soon, and he wanted to be reassured that I would be coming back. 'I shall save the newspapers for you as usual when you come back,' he said excitedly, gripping my arm. That was the moment when I knew that I *would* be back – although I didn't know precisely when. Wang's friend with the cigarette lighters appeared at that moment with a tray full of Zippos and I bought another one inscribed 'Hué 68–69' and 'For those who have to fight for it, Life has a flavour the protected will never know'. I liked that. I gave Wang the pretence of an uppercut and said goodbye to him with genuine affection.

My last morning I went for a short walk of rediscovery. I walked first up Dong Khoi Street towards the cathedral, bore left alongside it, and entered the area of tall trees that had been there long before I came to Saigon. Among the smart, newly painted houses and offices on my left had been the old Reuters office, where I had filed my copy to my newspaper in London, and further down, at the end of the main road, were the imposing gates of the former Presidential Palace.

In 1985, I remembered, the victory parade had passed down this wide street between these trees, where a small part of Saigon's population had stood with open mouths and unwaved red flags to see the troops goose-stepping by and the *ao dai*-ed girls from the North waving and smiling to their compatriots who looked frozen to the spot.

A character in a short story by Anton Chekhov I had been reading in my hotel remarked that King David had a ring with an inscription 'All things pass'. Life, too, will pass, he said. So perhaps one doesn't need anything but a sense of freedom, because when someone's free he needs nothing, nothing at all. This thought came to me under the trees by the cathedral as I prepared to leave.

But does everything pass away? I doubt it. If I wanted a ring I should choose the inscription 'Nothing passes away'. In particular, the sorrows of a long war like this one never pass away entirely; something of them remains forever.

I dearly hope to return to Vietnam; perhaps to visit Mme Bong; perhaps to visit her grave. Who knows?

The street was deserted now. Things had undoubtedly changed. A group of young men and women were half listening to a recording from a van with speakers that quacked out some political message. They were not really concentrating on what was being said.

Half my life seemed to have been spent here – between the cathedral, red brick and austere on my right, the iron gates of the palace on my left. Those things remained. I returned to my hotel the long way, strolling like a tourist down Pasteur Street, past big houses with high walls and rusting barbed wire. They remained, too, looking just as they had done at the height of war in 1965 when I first set foot in this city as quite a young man.

Appendix I

NO'S STORY

What follows is the story of one Vietnamese's – **No**'s – escape from Vietnam at the age of seventeen. In it **No** shows not only his father Ho Trang's chief characteristic sang-froid, he also demonstrates a surprising writing ability.

To show just what adventures and experiences these young Vietnamese boat people – now *Viet Kieu* – had to undergo after the communist victory of 1975, I append this personal account of fear, privation and ultimate success.

No ended up in Palawan Refugee Camp, like **Cun**. And eventually found himself in the house his far-seeing father, Ho Trang, had bought in Fairfax, Virginia. From there he joined the US Marine Corps, mainly, I think, because the Corps had a scheme that helped pay for his schooling.

What is missing from this modest account of a frightening escape is the sense of the downright terror of embarking illegally on a strange boat with a number of complete strangers, and heading to an unknown destination across dangerous seas. After all, **No** was a young boy at the time. They all were. **Bao**, **No**'s cousin and Minh's son, for example, was only fourteen when he crossed with **No**'s brother **Ly** into Thailand.

As I have said, this account was written two years after the event by **No**, and in America as a school exercise. His teacher – the one who first read it – said it was 'fascinating'. It *is* fascinating as it stands. Add three times or ten times the amount of fear in it, and the fascination becomes much, much greater.

And that is how, I believe, it really was: not only a fascinating, but also a terrifying experience. *Of course* it changed, as **No** himself says, 'many aspects of my life'. How could it not.

This is his story:

It was two years ago when Vietnam was no good for guys whose fathers were working for the South Vietnam government because these guys would have no chance of getting to colleges and are likely to be drafted for the front in Cambodia. I was one of these guys and there were no choices for me but leaving the country. Actually, it cost my mom most of her money to pay for my trip because it was illegal. Of course I had heard a lot about the danger, and the unpredictable outcomes of the trip, but I also wanted to take chance to change my life.

I still remember right now that at the night when I went, my mom was on a business trip, so she did not have a chance to prepare things for me. Fortunately, I realised that it was important enough for my own sake to pack enough food, water, and clothes for the trip. However, it was such a rush for me that I could not say goodbye to any of my friends, and I could only grab a few necessary things to go. At that night, I had to go to an appointed place where a group of strange people who had the same purpose as mine would meet to be ready to depart. Everybody was pretending to be cool, but I was sure that everyone had a mixed feeling of being worried, excited, and lonely. We did not talk to each other much because we were told to do so. After waiting there long enough for everybody to show up, we all left the scene to go to another place which was near a river where we could go by boat. There, we met several groups like ours, and they all looked and acted like we, the people in my group, did. Then, we broke up in small groups again to stay some where near that place for the night.

The next morning I had to wake up early, which was not a very nice thing for me to do, but I was awarded by a peaceful cruise across the long river with the people in my group, which included two beautiful girls, a young man, a woman who rowed the boat, and myself. The purpose of this trip was to get to the fourteen-meter long boat waiting for us in the far side of the river at 8 p.m. So far, it had been perfect for me, and I always thought that I was on my vacation because I had been eating much, sleeping well, rowing boat, watching the sunset, and talking to beautiful girls. The girls were pretty much used to this sort of thing because they had tried escaping many times before, and all we talked about was the experience of being at sea.

Finally we got to the fourteen-meter boat, and we got up there in a flash. It was extremely dark but I still realised that the boat was stacked with people and it took me fifteen minutes to find myself a spot to sit uncomfortably. I was tired but I could not sleep well that night at all for a simple reason: not enough spaces. In the morning, the sun came up and it was getting hotter and hotter because we did not have any covers in the top. People began to lessen themselves, and I finally had a rest stretchfully under the shining sun. I was told later that we were off the coast of VietNam then, that meant we would no longer be chased by the VietNamese coast guards. By noon, I went up to the front of the boat, where the concentration of people was less because the front was higher and it was considered dangerous. There, I could see the beautiful sea and the fish swimming along the boat. Later, more young boys joined me, and we all had a good time playing with the dolphins swimming along. These fish like to show off by jumping out of the water when they are cheered. Then, I realised that I had consumed all the food and water I brought along with me. The owners of the boat certainly had food and water for everybody, but the amount would be very limited, and I did not get any from them so far. Finally, food and water were given out to leaders of small groups and I had to get mine from my group, of course. When I finally got down from the front and found my group, everything was gone. Everybody even forgot that I was in their group. However, one of the girls in that group was kind enough to give me some water.

I then got back to the front of the boat to wait for the night to come. I kept on thinking about what had happened during the day, and found out that I was a zero on this boat. Nobody cared about me, and nobody would know if I was alright or not because everybody was not my mother, and for his or her own sake, everybody would try to survive in this boat first, and care for others later. It sounded like common sense, but it certainly took me a while to figure that out. I slept well that night after having a long conversation with a friend who was alone on the boat too. We told each other about things in our own schools, and it made me feel much better.

Things happened in the next day were like they did in the first day. We also met some foreign ships along the way. Every time we saw a ship, we usually shouted, waved and asked to be rescued, but we always got no response.

The next day, the only thing different from the day before was that the food was fish instead of anything else. I always do not eat fish, and I did not break my rule on that day either.

Things turned out to be boring until the next afternoon when we met the Thai fishermen. The Thai fishermen usually go fishing in groups, that means if you randomly see one Thai fishing boat, you will be able to see about ten or more Thai boats near the one you first see. The Thais were kind enough to tell us that we lost our way, and threw us food and water enough for at least another week. We also asked them to pull us to Malaysia, because one out of three engines was broken, but I thought that was too much the Thais said they had to do some fishing first. Off we went under a new direction given by the Thais. Then I had a chance to drink as much as I could, and I felt like having enough energy to go for another week. Later in that afternoon, we found out through the binoculars that one of the Thai fishing boats followed us. We kept asking ourselves why and finally came up with the answer that the Thai wanted to help us pulling our boat to Malaysia. The Thai were not gods. As a matter of fact, one of the boats came after us in a rush, and about ten of them armed with long knives got in our boat and robbed every valuable things they could find. The women on the boat were so panicked in that they just stuck anything nasty they could find on their faces to make themselves look ugly. One of the Thai was standing just next to me holding a knife. By looking at his eyes and being pushed by my curiosity, I assumed that the man was no harm at all. Thus, I started asking him what the whole thing was about, and he responded by swinging his sword round and saying, 'OK . . . OK . . . USA . . . OK . . . USA!!!' I could not help laughing out loud. Finally, their boat also got away in a rush without harming anybody. We then kept going on the old direction and finally found a big ship with guns coming towards us. That ship was a French military ship guarding another bigger ship named *Cap Anamur*. These ships were looking for all the refugee boats to rescue them. Everybody in my boat was feeling like being reborn . . .

I am sure that the story above will amaze some of the people who read it. I tell this experience to a lot of my friends, and I always get the same kind of reaction: fascination. But the experience is not fiction. In fact, it changed many aspects of my life.

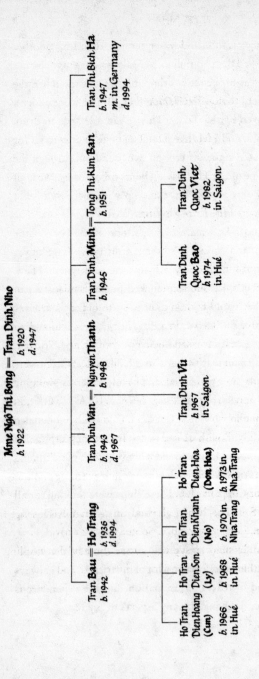

Mme Ngô Thị Bong = **Tran Dinh Nho**
b. 1922   b. 1920
                                        d. 1947

Tran **Bau** = **Ho Trang**
b. 1942   b. 1936
                  d. 1994

Tran Dinh **Van** = **Nguyen Thanh**
b. 1943   b. 1948
d. 1967

Tran Dinh **Minh** = **Tong Thi Kim Ban**
b. 1945   b. 1951

Tran Thi **Bich Ha**
b. 1947
m. in Germany
d. 1994

Ho Tran
Dien Hoang
(**Cun**)
b. 1966
in Huế

Ho Tran
Dien Son
(**Ly**)
b. 1968
in Huế

Ho Tran
Dien Khanh
(**No**)
b. 1970 in
Nha Trang

Ho Tran
Dien Hoa.
(**Don Hoa**)
b. 1973 in.
Nha Trang

Tran Dinh **Vu**
b. 1967
in Saigon

Tran Dinh
Quoc **Bao**
b. 1974
in Huế

Tran Dinh
Quoc **Viet**
b. 1982
in Saigon

Appendix II

FAMILY DATA

Ho Trang's family

HO TRANG

Born on 14 July 1936 in Hué.

Arrived in the US in 1984. While attending Northern Virginia Community College for two years had a number of odd jobs. Obtained an Associate Degree in Electrical Engineering. Often held two jobs to support family. Situation eased slightly when **Cun** and **No** arrived in 1987. In 1990 obtained job as a mechanical technician at the Washington Metro Co.; higher salary provided more stability and benefits for the family. In the same year he was able to buy the house in Fairfax, Virginia, in which the family still lives. Stayed in this job until he fell seriously ill with cancer in 1994. Died in that year.

TRAN BAU (Ho Trang's wife)

Born on 17 January 1942 in Hué.

Arrived in the US in 1991 when allowed to join family; has lived with the family in Fairfax ever since. Soon after her arrival worked for one year at a McDonald's restaurant. Since 1992 has been working for Guest Service Inc. as a food service person.

HO TRAN DIEN HOANG (nicknamed **Cun**)
    Born on 6 January 1966 in Hué.
    Arrived in the US in 1987. A college drop-out; has become a mailman,
    working 40–56 hours a week.

HO TRAN DIEN SON (nicknamed **Ly**)
    Born on 28 March 1968 in Hué.
    Arrived in the US in 1990. Goes to Northern Virginia Community
    College, and works part-time as a produce clerk.

HO TRAN DIEN KHANH (nicknamed **No**)
    Born on 8 November 1970 in Nha Trang.
    Arrived in the US in 1987. Went to George Mason University, joined
    the US Marines; obtained a BA in Computer Science, and now
    works as a computer programmer and software analyst. A US Marine
    Reserve.

HO TRAN DIEN HOA (nicknamed **Don Hoa**)
    Born on 8 August 1973 in Nha Trang.
    Arrived in the US in 1989. Senior in Computer Science at George
    Mason University; joined US Marines and remains a US Marine
    Reserve. Works part-time as a cashier clerk.

Minh's family

TRAN DINH MINH

Born 29 January 1945 in Hué.

Arrived with his wife in the US under the ODP on 28 February 1991.

Works full-time as a custodian for the Fairfax County Public School and part-time as a salad-bar clerk for Giant Food supermarket.

TONG THI KIM BAN (Minh's wife)

Born 20 October 1951 in Hué.

Arrived in the US on 28 February 1991. Works in a McDonald's restaurant.

TRAN DINH QUOC BAO (nicknamed **Na**)

Born 20 July 1974 in Hué.

Arrived in the US on 11 April 1990. Majoring in Pharmacy at George Mason University and works part-time as a pharmacy clerk at Giant Food.

TRAN DINH QUOC VIET (nicknamed **Tin**)

Born 8 August 1982 in Saigon.

Arrived in the US on 28 February 1991. Ninth Grade at Fairfax High School.

Qué's family

Qué and his family arrived in the US on 21 February 1995 under the Orderly Departure Programme.

DANG VAN QUE
  Born 1 January 1946.
  Currently studying English.

TONG THI CAM HONG (Qué's wife)
  Born 2 July 1947.
  Works as a maid for State Plaza Hotel in Washington, D.C.

DANG DONG AN
  Born 6 January 1974.
  Works for On Site Sourcing.

DANG THAI HOA
  Born 22 June 1975.
  Works for US Spring in telemarketing.

DANG THI KIM GIAO
  Born 19 December 1982.
  Attends Lincoln Junior High School in Washington, D.C.

READ MORE IN PENGUIN

In every corner of the world, on every subject under the sun, Penguin represents quality and variety – the very best in publishing today.

For complete information about books available from Penguin – including Puffins, Penguin Classics and Arkana – and how to order them, write to us at the appropriate address below. Please note that for copyright reasons the selection of books varies from country to country.

In the United Kingdom: Please write to *Dept. EP, Penguin Books Ltd, Bath Road, Harmondsworth, West Drayton, Middlesex UB7 ODA*

In the United States: Please write to *Consumer Sales, Penguin Putnam Inc., P.O. Box 999, Dept. 17109, Bergenfield, New Jersey 07621-0120.* VISA and MasterCard holders call 1-800-253-6476 to order Penguin titles

In Canada: Please write to *Penguin Books Canada Ltd, 10 Alcorn Avenue, Suite 300, Toronto, Ontario M4V 3B2*

In Australia: Please write to *Penguin Books Australia Ltd, P.O. Box 257, Ringwood, Victoria 3134*

In New Zealand: Please write to *Penguin Books (NZ) Ltd, Private Bag 102902, North Shore Mail Centre, Auckland 10*

In India: Please write to *Penguin Books India Þvt Ltd, 210 Chiranjiv Tower, 43 Nehru Place, New Delhi 110 019*

In the Netherlands: Please write to *Penguin Books Netherlands bv, Postbus 3507, NL-1001 AH Amsterdam*

In Germany: Please write to *Penguin Books Deutschland GmbH, Metzlerstrasse 26, 60594 Frankfurt am Main*

In Spain: Please write to *Penguin Books S. A., Bravo Murillo 19, 1° B, 28015 Madrid*

In Italy: Please write to *Penguin Italia s.r.l., Via Benedetto Croce 2, 20094 Corsico, Milano*

In France: Please write to *Penguin France, Le Carré Wilson, 62 rue Benjamin Baillaud, 31500 Toulouse*

In Japan: Please write to *Penguin Books Japan Ltd, Kaneko Building, 2-3-25 Koraku, Bunkyo-Ku, Tokyo 112*

In South Africa: Please write to *Penguin Books South Africa (Pty) Ltd, Private Bag X14, Parkview, 2122 Johannesburg*

BY THE SAME AUTHOR

'Intrepid, reflective and gregarious . . . plainly a man in a million and a writer in two' – Bernard Levin in the *Observer*

From Sea to Shining Sea

'He catches the mind's eye of the reader very deftly . . . and, without losing his sense of irony, gives us a genuine account of the tragedy and the pathos, as well as the optimism and bravery, that created American civilization' – Christopher Hitchens in the *Mail on Sunday*

In Search of Conrad

Joint Winner of the 1992 Thomas Cook Travel Book Award

'Part mariner's log and part detective story, it brilliantly evokes the Far-Eastern landscapes fixed forever in our imaginations by Conrad's novels . . . the most pleasurable and exciting book I have read this year' – J. G. Ballard in the *Daily Telegraph*

Slow Boats to China

Gavin Young's bestselling account of his extraordinary journey in small boats through the Mediterranean, the Red Sea, the Indian Ocean and the Malaya and China Seas to China.

and

Slow Boats Home
Worlds Apart
Beyond Lion Rock: The Story of Cathay Pacific Airways